W9-BKI-963

THE HOW AND WHY WONDER BOOK OF

OUR EARTH

By FELIX SUTTON
Illustrated by JOHN HULL
Editorial Production: DONALD D. WOLF

Edited under the supervision of
Dr. Paul E. Blackwood
Washington, D. C.

Text and illustrations approved by
Oakes A. White
Brooklyn Children's Museum
Brooklyn, New York

GROSSET & DUNLAP • Publishers • NEW YORK

Introduction

Earth, at this writing, is still the home of all known people. And though it is fun to speculate about life on other planets in our solar system and in other star systems, most of us will continue to live on earth. So it makes good sense to learn as much about our home planet as we can.

This *How and Why Wonder Book* is a good guide to learning more about the earth. It deals with a variety of topics and answers many questions. How was the earth formed? What is inside the earth? What causes volcanoes? What do fossils tell us? How are mountains and seas formed? Indeed, the book is really *geology,* the study of the earth, made easy.

A fascinating aspect about the study of the earth is that we can see today the same processes that have been going on for millions and millions of years in the past. Reading the book gives one a feeling of living with the history of the earth and learning about it at the same time.

Parents, teachers and children alike will profit from reading the book. It is surely an essential addition to the growing *How and Why Wonder Book* library of every young scientist.

Paul E. Blackwood

Dr. Blackwood is a professional employee in the U. S. Office of Education. This book was edited by him in his private capacity and no official support or endorsement by the Office of Education is intended or should be inferred.

Library of Congress Catalog Card Number: 60-51567

1971 Printing

Published simultaneously in Canada. Printed in the United States of America.

Contents

Beginning of the Earth

How was the earth formed?

Scientists believe that about a hundred billion years ago the earth, the sun, and all the planets of the solar system were nothing but a cloud of cold dust particles swirling through empty space.

Gradually, these particles were attracted to each other and came together to form a huge, spinning disk. As it spun, the disk separated into rings, and the furious motion made the particles white-hot.

The center of the disk became the sun, and the particles in the outer rings turned into large fiery balls of gas ana molten liquid. Then they began to cool and condense and take on solid form. And at last, some four or five billion years ago, they became Earth, Mars, Venus and the other planets.

What is the earth like inside?

Essentially, the earth is constructed something like a baseball. If you were to cut a baseball in two, you would see that it has a core of solid rubber. Wrapped around this inner core are a great many layers of heavy string. This

string binding is solid, yet it is not as solid as the rubber core, for it will give and sometimes alter its shape under pressure. The outer covering is a thin layer of horsehide which holds in all the rest of the ball.

The solid-rock covering of the earth, called the *crust,* is between ten and thirty miles thick — much thinner in proportion than the horsehide covering of the baseball.

Under this crust is a thick layer of a different kind of rock, which is known as the earth's *mantle.* The rock of the mantle is solid, but it is solid in the same way that the string wrapping of the ball is solid. Under pressure it will move slightly and change its shape. The mantle extends to a depth of 1,800 miles.

Enclosed by the mantle is the earth's *core.* Unlike the center of a baseball, the center of the earth is made up of two parts: an *outer* core and an *inner*

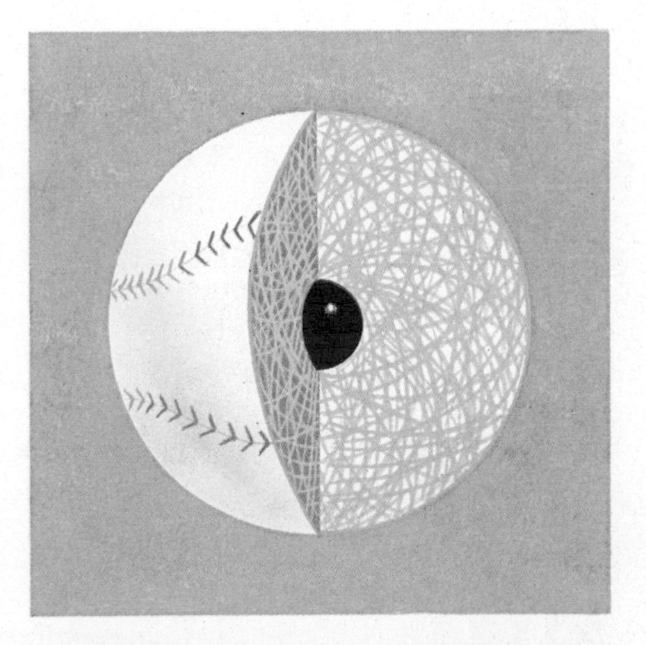

As the illustrations indicate, the construction of the earth may be compared to that of a baseball. The earth's covering is called the *crust.* Under it is the *mantle.* Within that is the core (center of the earth).

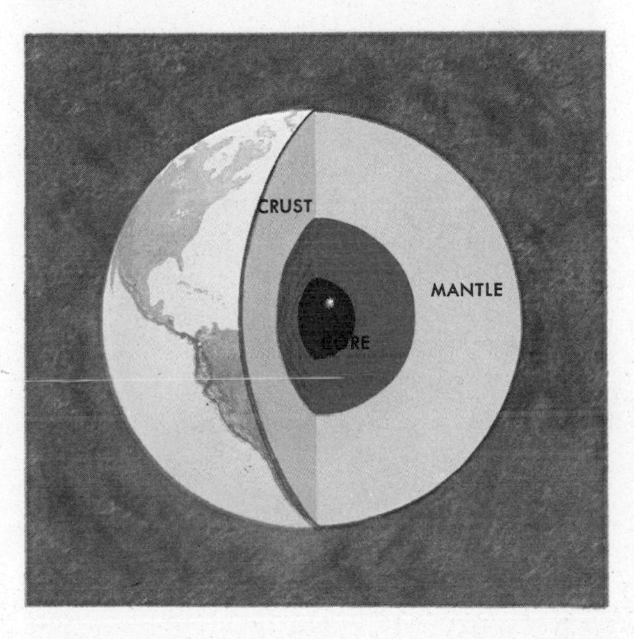

core. Both are composed of metal — mostly iron, with some nickel — but the outer core is liquid and the inner core is solid. At the very center of the core, the temperature is about 8,000 degrees — not much less than the temperature on the surface of the sun.

The total distance from the earth's surface to its center averages approximately 3,960 miles.

How can we tell what the inside of the earth is like?

No scientific instrument has ever penetrated more than two or three miles into the earth, How, then, are we able to tell what the inside of the earth is like? The answer is: by the action of *earthquakes*.

Thousands of earthquakes occur every year in many parts of the world. Most of them are too slight to cause damage, but all of them send out shock waves that penetrate all through the earth, even the deepest parts.

These earthquake waves are of two basic kinds: P (primary) waves, and S (secondary) waves. P waves travel faster than S waves. P waves go through liquids, but S waves can't. The speed of both P and S waves vary according to the depth of the earth they have penetrated. Both behave differently when passing through different kinds of rocks.

When these waves come back to the surface, they are recorded on a delicate instrument called a *seismograph*

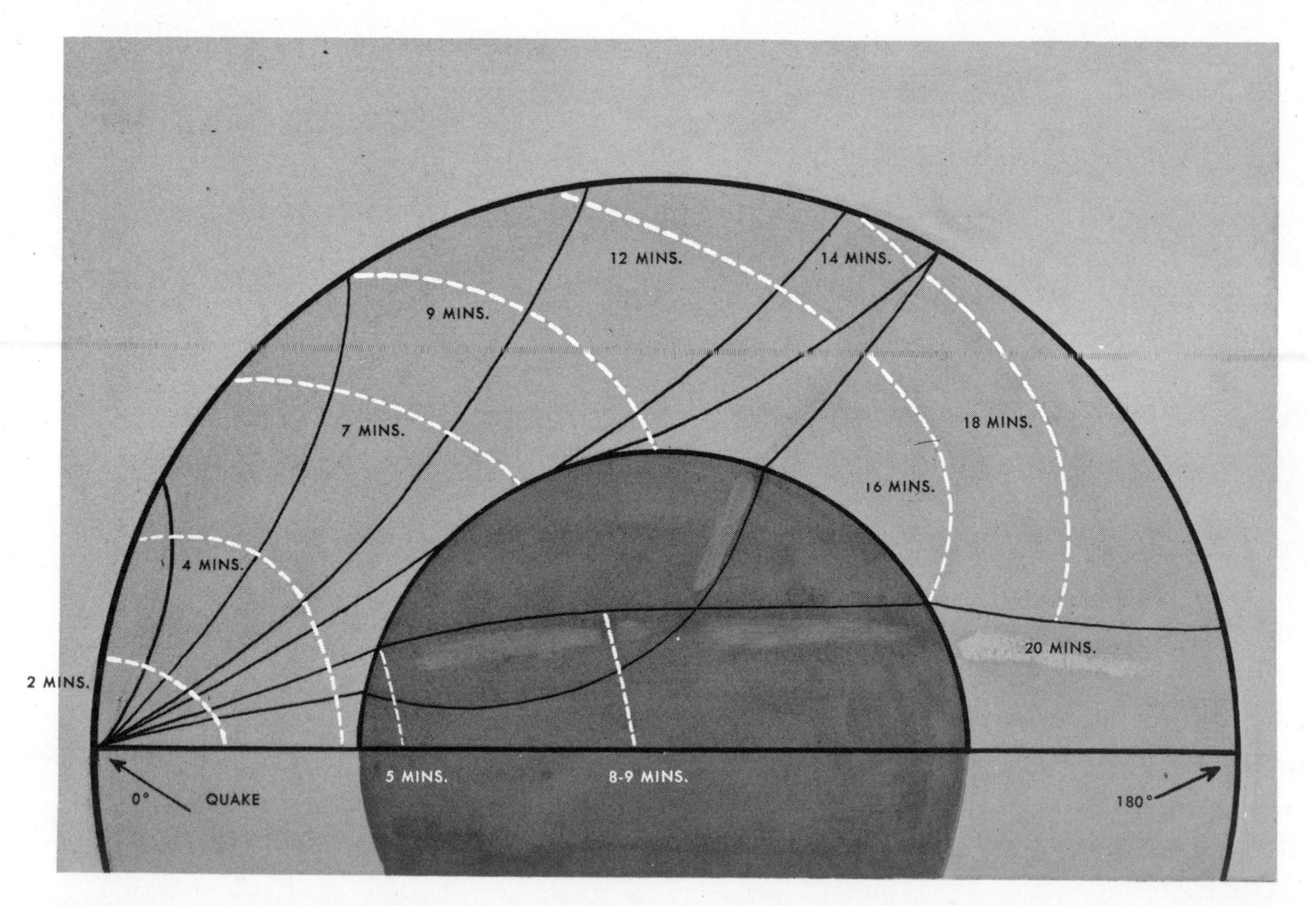

By studying the speed and behavior of earthquake waves, scientists can tell what the inside of the earth is like.

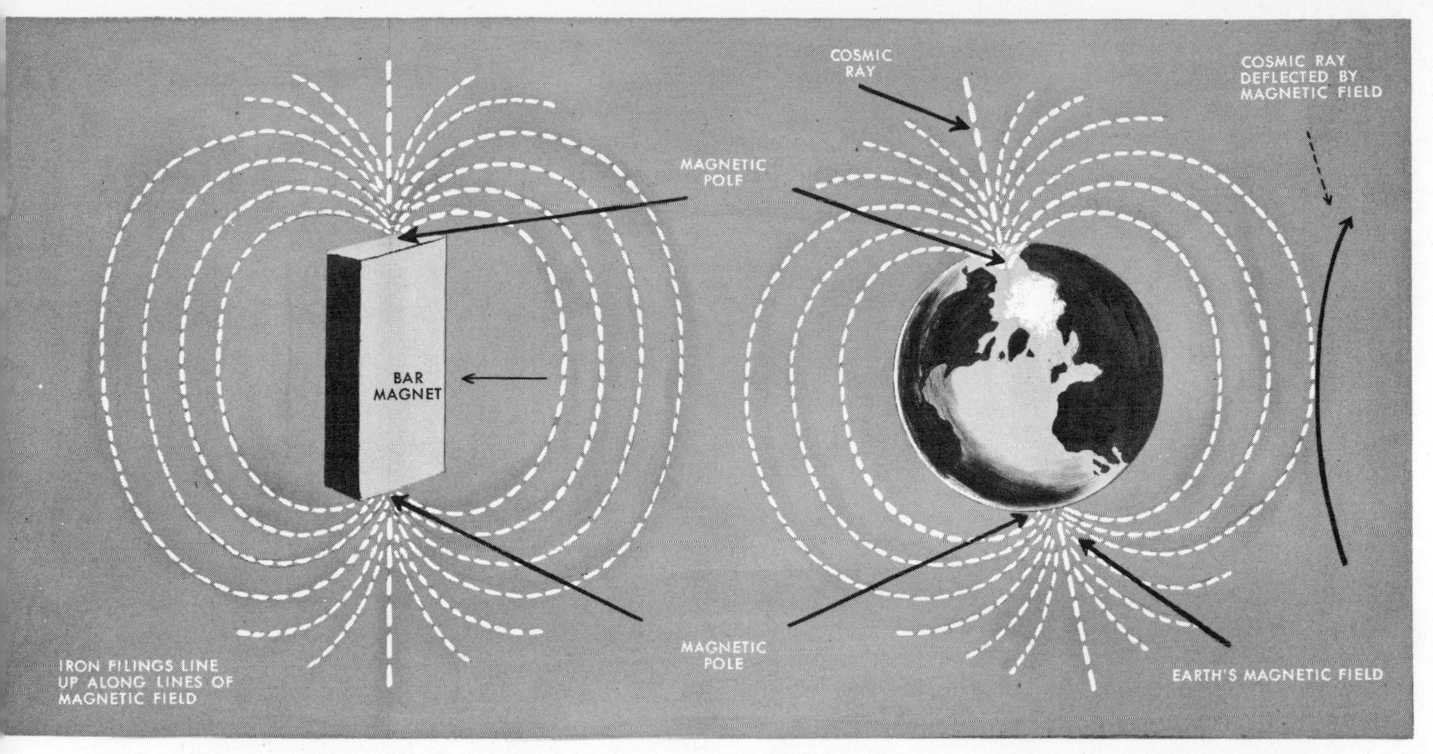

These diagrams show the magnetic field of a bar magnet (left) and the magnetic field of the earth (right). Note that the North and South Magnetic Poles are not in the same positions as the geographic North and South Poles.

(SIZE-mo-graf). And it is by studying the speed and behavior of the P and S waves — the distance they have traveled from their point of origin, the depths at which they have been reflected and bent, and the time it has taken for them to make their journey — that scientists are able to determine what the inside of the earth is like.

Why does a compass point north?

The fact that the earth is a gigantic magnet was discovered more than a thousand years ago. But people did not know what they had discovered. They knew that if a needle was stroked by a *loadstone* (a mineral, which is a natural magnet), the needle would always point north. But they supposed that the needle was attracted by the North Star. We know now that the needle is attracted by the North Magnetic Pole.

We know today that the magnetic pole is as much as a thousand miles from the true, or geographic, pole. But the two poles are always just about the same distance apart.

What causes the magnetic field?

There are a great many things about the earth's magnetism that scientists still do not know. But the most widely accepted theory is that the magnetic field is set up by electric currents deep within the earth's liquid core. These currents are created when minerals of different temperatures and different electrical properties come together. This means that the inside of the earth is a huge, natural generator, which is constantly turning mechanical energy (the earth's rotation and the movement of the liquid core) into electrical energy. And, of course, we know that all magnetic fields are the

result of electric currents, and all electric currents are surrounded by magnetic fields.

How can you make your own compass?

Take an ordinary needle from your mother's sewing basket and stroke it a few times — always in the same direction — with a toy magnet which you can buy for a few cents in any toy store. Now cut a very thin slice from an ordinary bottle cork, and float it on top of a glass dish full of water. Place the needle on the cork, and it will make the cork swing around until the needle is pointing north and south.

Have the North and South poles ever changed their positions?

Geologists today have been able to ascertain a fact which is quite surprising to many people: throughout millions of centuries, the north and south magnetic poles have actually wandered about the earth! Half a billion years ago, the north magnetic pole was near the equator in the eastern Pacific. A hundred and seventy million years ago, early in the Age of Dinosaurs, it lay in Siberia. There have been times, also, when it was located in Korea, the middle of the North Atlantic Ocean, and possibly Africa. Even more remarkable, the north and south poles have changed places! In the past eighty million years, it is estimated that 171 such reversals

From measurements of the magnetism of ancient rocks, as well as from studies of fossil animals and plants, scientists know that the geographic North and South Poles of the earth have changed positions.

have occurred, though no one knows why it happened.

We know this from lava containing grains of the mineral magnetite (or loadstone) that once flowed from prehistoric volcanoes. When the rock is extremely hot, the grains are not magnetized, since high temperatures demagnetize magnetic materials. When the lava cools, though, the grains of magnetite reach a certain temperature (called the Curie point) at which magnetism is restored. As the lava hardens into rock, the earth's magnetic field lines up the grains in the current north-south direction, but when the lava hardens completely, the grains no longer move around.

Thus, when scientists examine the rock formed from lava, thousands of "compass needles" (the grains of magnetite) point to where the north and south magnetic poles were when the rock was formed.

Upheavals in the Earth

What causes earthquakes?

Most of the time, the surface of the earth is firm and steady. But sometimes the ground shakes and trembles, jarring masses of rocks loose from mountainsides, causing *fissures* (narrow openings) in the surface, and knocking down buildings in cities and towns.

We know that the thin outer crust of the earth is formed of uneven layers of different kinds of rocks. These rocks are subject to constant pressures, not

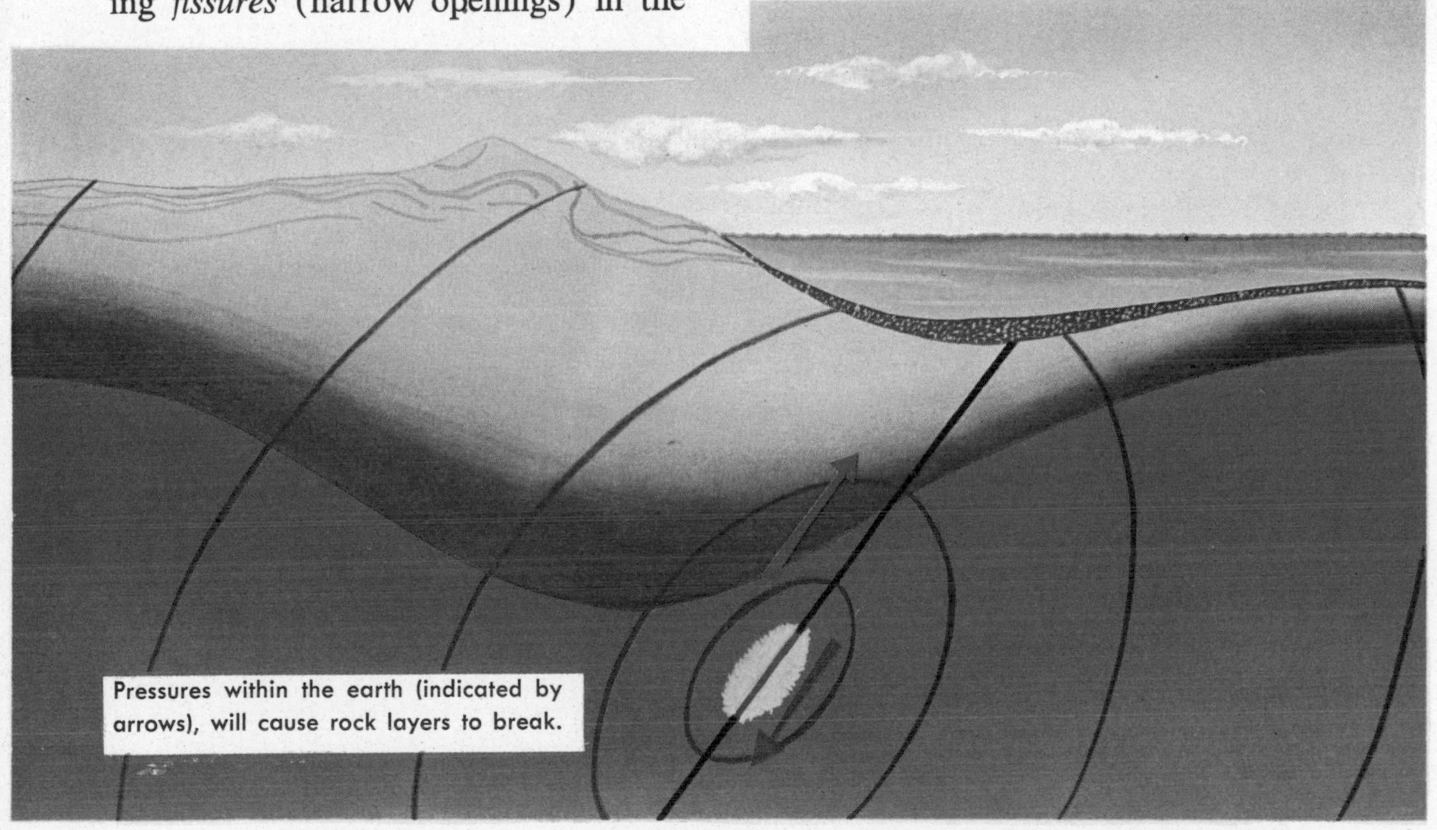

Pressures within the earth (indicated by arrows), will cause rock layers to break.

only from the rock layers that lie above them, but also from forces within the earth itself. These pressures bend the rocks and cause them to change shape.

If these pressures are great enough, the rock layers may suddenly break — in the same way that a stick will give just so far when you bend it in your hands, and then suddenly snap in two.

When this happens, the rocks break apart and snap back just as the two broken ends of the stick do. This sudden snap jars the earth's crust and causes it to shake. And this movement is called an earthquake.

How were the mountains formed?

If we were able to slice open a mountain range such as the Rockies, the Andes or the Alps, we would see that the layers of rocks had been broken, bent and crumpled. We would also find that many of the rock layers that now tower thousands of feet above sea level were once formed at the bottom

of the ocean. We know that this happened because the fossil remains of sea animals have been found in rocks on the topmost peaks.

From these facts, we conclude that the mountains were formed from the rocks of ancient sea floors — and that powerful forces from within the earth broke and folded and raised these rocks into their present positions.

When the mountain ranges rose slowly out of the sea in this way, other forces began at once to go to work. Swift-flowing streams and slow-moving glaciers began tearing the mountains away. (This process of wearing away — usually, wearing away land by the action of moving water — is called *erosion.*) Landslides moved material from higher places to lower ones. As soon as the mountains rose above the sea, erosion began to destroy them.

Geologists believe that the surface of the earth is constantly changing in this way — that the earth's crust is in constant motion, like the waves on the

Aerial view of volcanic ridges and mountains

surface of a sea. But instead of rising up and leveling off again in a split-second, as sea waves do, the movement of the "waves" of the earth's surface is measured in terms of hundreds of millions of years.

What causes volcanoes?

The solid rock layers which form the earth's crust are thicker in some places than in others, and directly underneath them, the earth's internal temperature is hot enough to melt rock. This molten rock is known as *magma* (MAG-ma).

At certain places under the crust, magma collects in reservoirs or pools. As this magma wells up out of the insides of the earth, it pushes gases ahead of it. As the gases become more and more tightly compressed, they exert a tremendous pressure against the underside of the crust. If this occurs at a place where the crust is weak, or where an ancient earthquake has created a break in the rock, the mixture of gas and magma breaks through the crack and erupts on the surface in the form of lava.

As the lava gushes out through the crack in the earth, it cools and solidifies and, in time, forms a cone around the opening that grows higher and higher. In the end it becomes a volcanic mountain.

Sometimes a volcano keeps erupting and throwing out great clouds of smoke and ashes and streams of lava for many years at a time. Then, when enough of the internal gases have been released to ease the pressure from far underground, the eruption stops. The lava

Eruption of a volcano: Mount Popocatepetl in Mexico.

inside the cone then cools and plugs up the crack in the crust. Often, many years later, the pressure builds up again, blows out the plug of solid lava, and the volcano erupts once more.

Why does a geyser throw out steam?

Geysers might be described as small distant cousins of volcanoes, for they too are created by the earth's internal heat.

Water from the surface penetrates deep down into long vertical cracks in the underlying rock which act as natural "water pipes." When this water sinks deep enough, the heat of the earth causes it to boil. Then the whole column of water and steam shoots up out of the top of the "pipe" to produce the beautiful fountain display for which geysers are famous. After the geyser has erupted, the whole process begins all over again.

Geysers exist in only three places in the world: Iceland, New Zealand and Yellowstone National Park in the western United States. Of these, the Yellowstone geysers are the most numerous and most spectacular. Yellowstone's most famous geyser, "Old Faithful," erupts at fairly regular intervals of about an hour.

How can you make your own geyser?

You can make your own geyser by putting a funnel mouth-down in a saucepan. Fill the pan with water until only the neck sticks out. Place a spoon or some other small object under one lip of the funnel so that the water can get under it. Now put the pan on a fire. As the

Eruption of a geyser: "Old Faithful" in Yellowstone.

water at the bottom of the pan boils, it is forced out of the top of the tube, in the same way that a geyser erupts.

How were the seas formed?

As the molten rock that formed the surface of the young earth began to cool and solidify, gases bubbled up out of the seething interior of the globe and escaped into the atmosphere that surrounded it. Here they collected together into great clouds of water vapor. When these clouds became heavy enough, the moisture condensed and began to fall back to earth in the form of rain. But the surface was still red-hot, and as the falling raindrops approached it, they boiled away and returned into the upper atmosphere as vapor.

You can see how this happened by heating a griddle on a stove. When the griddle is hot, slowly drop water on it from an eye-dropper. You will see that as the drops of water touch the hot surface of the griddle, they immediately boil away as steam vapor.

So, for probably millions of years,

Thick rain clouds surrounded the earth for millions of years. When the earth cooled, they burst in a great rain, creating massive valleys which became seas.

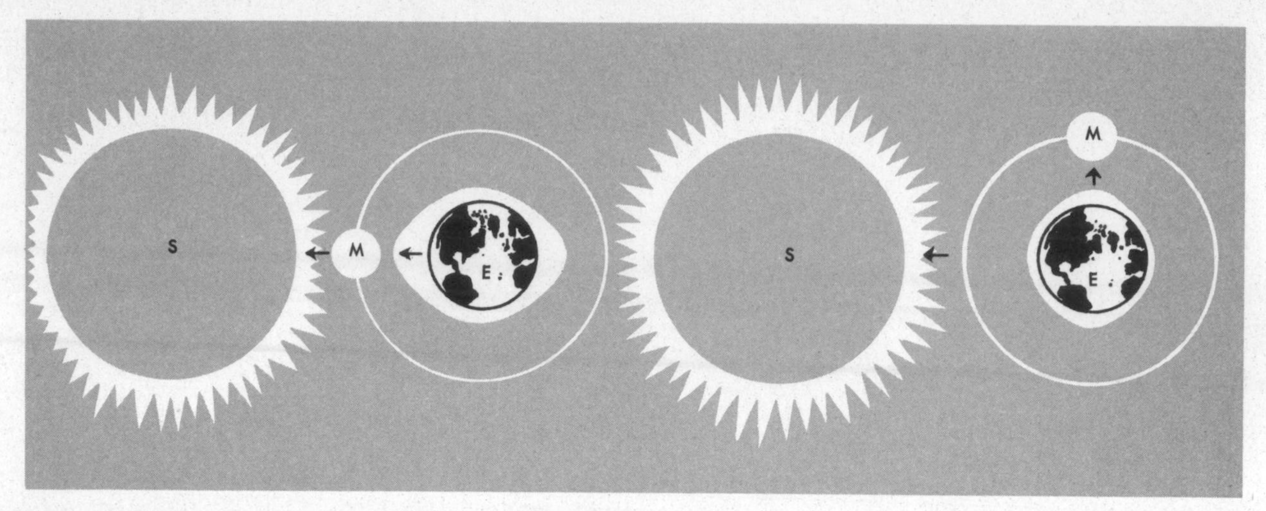

Spring tides: Sun, earth and moon are in a straight line. Neap tides: The moon is at right angles to the sun.

the earth was surrounded by a heavy blanket of rain clouds that was many miles in thickness — endlessly condensing, falling as rain, and then being boiled back up into the sky again.

Then, slowly, the earth's crust hardened and cooled. And at last the surface rocks became so cool that their heat would no longer boil water. And the rain that had been collecting for all these millions of years up in the thick blanket of clouds began to fall in a never-ending torrent.

For hundreds, perhaps thousands of years, the rains came pouring down in a solid cloudburst. They leveled off mountain ranges and cut great valleys in the earth. And when at last the deluge had slowed and stopped, the lowest levels of the earth's wrinkled and folded crust had been filled up with water. These were the first oceans.

Why is sea water salty?

The rivers that flow across the face of the land carry millions of tons of silt and sediment down to the oceans each year. These dissolved materials contain nearly all the minerals that are found in the earth, including vast quantities of salt.

The heat of the sun evaporates, or dries up, some of the water on the sea's surface and sends it back into the air as water vapor. There it condenses into clouds and falls back to earth as rain or snow.

But in this process of evaporation, the minerals are left behind in the oceans. Some of them, like iron and calcium, are absorbed by the sea's animals and plants. But the salt is not used by either the animals or plants and so it continues to collect in the sea in ever-increasing quantities.

What causes the tides?

Anyone who has been to the seashore has seen the daily ebb and flow of the tides. At certain times of day the level of the water rises, usually ten or twenty feet. Then it recedes and leaves a long, empty stretch of beach behind it. This is caused by the gravitational pull of the sun and the moon.

During the periods of new moon and

full moon, the sun, the earth and the moon are all in a straight line. And so both moon and sun work together to cause extremely high tides, known as "spring tides."

On the other hand, when the moon is in the first and third quarter, it is at right angles to the sun. Under these conditions, the pull of the sun and moon tend to offset each other, and thus the tides are lower. These are called "neap tides."

But there are other puzzling things about the tides that cannot be explained by the simple force of gravity.

Around most of the Atlantic, the tides come and go twice a day. But in parts of the Pacific and Indian Oceans, the tide comes in only once a day. At Nantucket Island, off the coast of Massachusetts, high tide changes the level of the water only about one foot. But in the Bay of Fundy, only a few hundred miles north of Nantucket, the water level changes as much as forty feet.

These differences are caused by the irregularities of the ocean floor.

The floor of the sea is not flat, but instead is composed of vast basins, some broader and deeper than others. In these basins the sea water goes back and forth like the water in a dishpan or bathtub when it is disturbed. But water in a bathtub reacts more violently than water in a shallow pan. And, in the same way, the disturbance created by the pull of the moon and sun on the ocean's waters, is always much greater where the ocean basin is deeper.

Souvenirs of the Past

How were sea fossils made?

Half a billion years ago there was no life at all on the land, only in the warm waters of the seas. And even in the sea there were no types of fishes as we know them today. There were only worms, snails, sponges and primitive crablike creatures.

When these animals died, their bodies sank into the silt and mud of the ocean floor, and the currents covered them up with still more mud. Then, as thousands and millions of years went by, the sea bottom slowly hardened into rock. The bodies of the animals decayed and disappeared, but the remarkably detailed outlines of their forms were preserved forever in the rock.

Trilobite (an extinct sea animal) embedded in rock.

Then pressures from inside the earth gradually bent the layers of rock and lifted them out of the water. They rose up at the rate of one or two inches every few thousand years, and at last became the tops of mountains. And scientists found the fossil remains of the long-dead sea creatures, not on the floor of the ocean into which they had sunk, but on high mountain peaks.

What do we learn from fossils?

It is by studying these fossils of animals and plants that we are able to learn about the kind of life that existed on our earth when it was very young.

By studying fossils, we now know that the first life probably appeared on earth about two billion years ago in the form of a kind of algae, the green scum that we often see on the surface of ponds in the summertime.

Then, about five or six hundred million years ago, came the first primitive forms of animal life such as worms and jellyfishes. Following them were the fishes, the first animals with backbones. And then, something like two hundred million years ago, the first amphibians (am-FIB-ians) waddled out of the sea onto the land, developed lungs and legs, and became the first air-breathing animals.

The slow development of life went on — of the reptiles (including dinosaurs) and of the mammals (including man). And the whole story of life is there for us to see and study in the "picture book" of the fossil-bearing rocks.

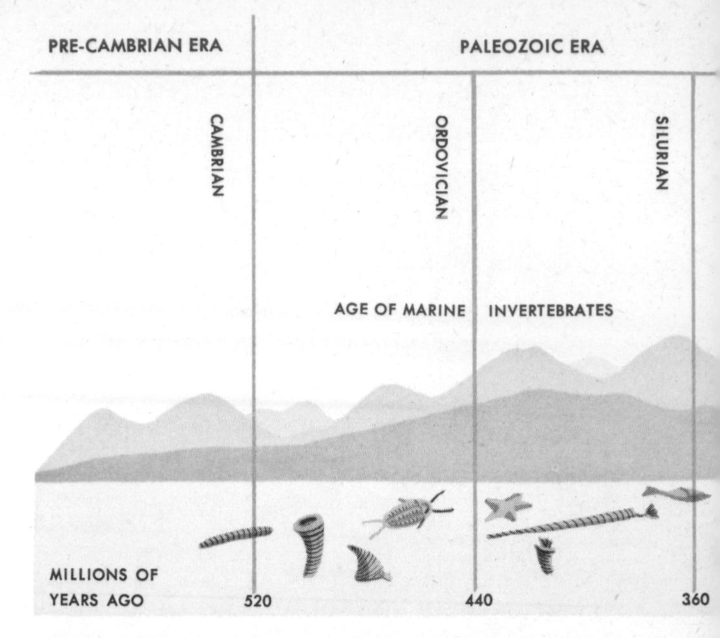

The ages of the earth are divided into eras of geological history. These eras are further divided into periods which designate the system of rocks formed during each period. The chart above also indicates the form of life dominant in each phase of history.

Has the earth always been the same?

The face of our earth is changing every day, just as it has been changing ever since the dawn of creation. If we look closely, we can see evidences of this ever-present change all around us. After a heavy rain, the water of a stream is muddy. This means that the rain has washed away soil from one place and the stream is carrying it to another. Slowly but surely, the hills through which the stream flows are being worn down and leveled off.

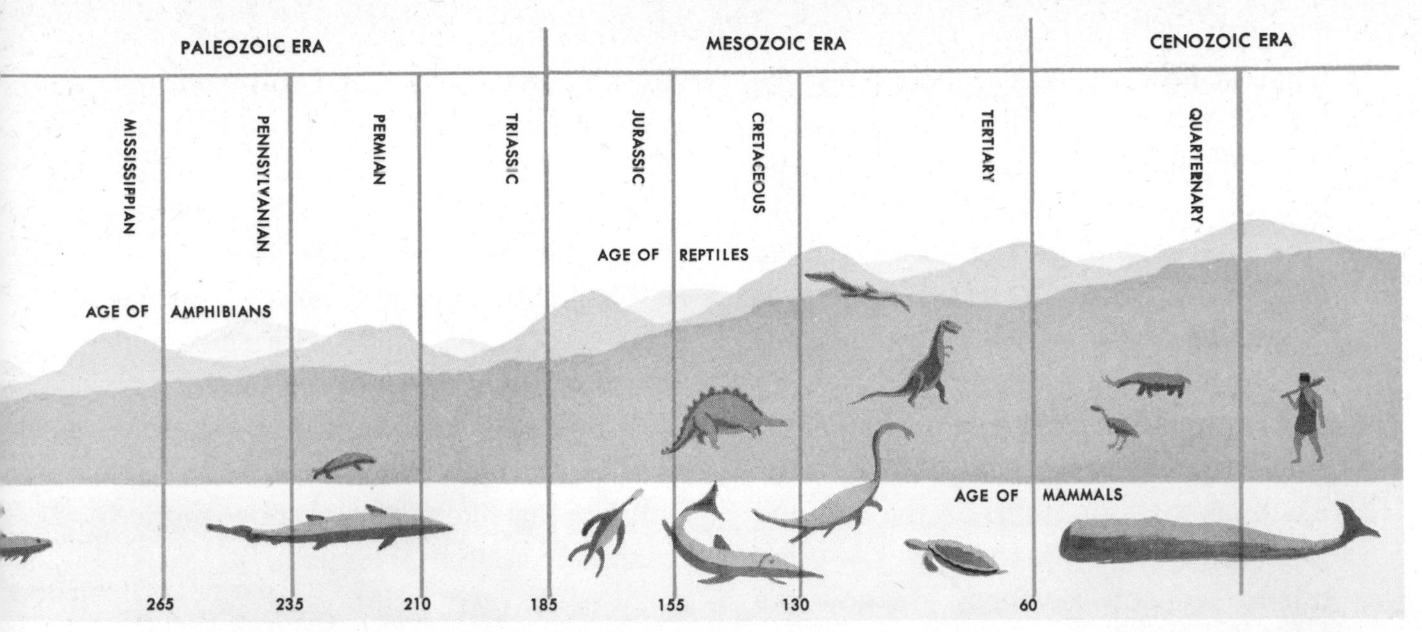

During periods of the earth's geological history, great land masses probably connected (from left to right), Siberia and Alaska, South America and Africa, England and Scandinavia. Fossil evidence supports this.

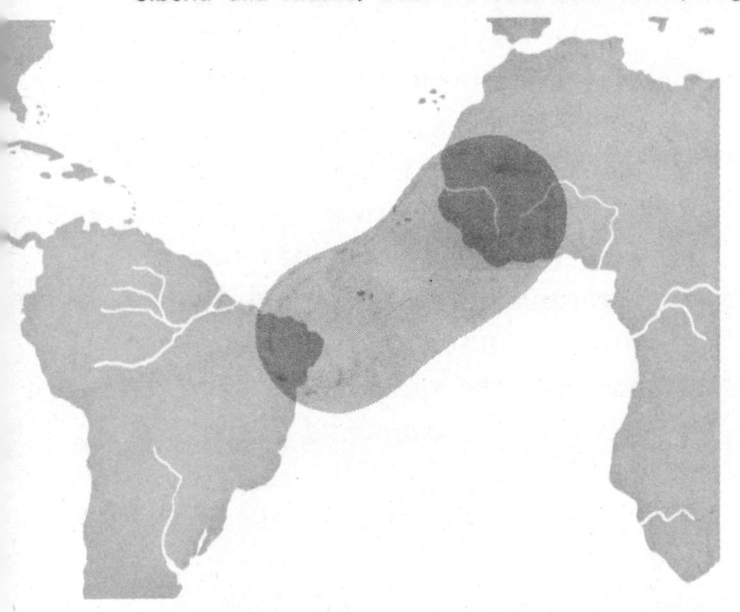

In the same way, the tumbling waves of the oceans wash away the sands of the beaches and alter the shape of the shorelines.

Again, geologists can read the history of the changing continents in the "picture book" of the rocks.

Fossils of animals that once lived on land have been found at the bottom of the sea. This indicates that these particular sea bottoms were at one time a part of the dry land. And this seems reasonable, since we have learned that the tops of many mountains once lay at the bottom of the sea.

What was the earth like long ago?

A careful study of these fossil clues has given scientists the following picture of what our earth must have been like at various periods of geologic history.

At one time, a bridge of land probably connected northern Europe with Greenland. Another such land bridge possibly extended between Spain and what is now the eastern coast of the United States. At still another stage in the long history of the changing continents, Africa, Australia and South America were all part of the same mass of land — and forests of fern trees grew across what are today thousands of miles of open water.

Two hundred million years ago, most of North America was under water. Then, as the mountains on the east and west emerged above the waves, a great inland sea covered what are now the midwestern states.

Then, much later, during the Stone Age, many thousands of years ago, the British Isles and the southern tip of Sweden were connected to the continent of Europe. A vast swampy plain filled in what are now the North Sea and the English Channel. The Thames River in England and the Rhine in Germany flowed together to create one mighty stream.

At about this time, too, Siberia was probably connected to Alaska by a land bridge across the Bering Strait. It is believed that early man must have migrated across this bridge from Asia to become the ancestors of the American Indians. Mammoths, the huge, furry forerunners of elephants, apparently took this same route in their travels, for their bones have been found in the American deserts.

What causes a glacier?

A *glacier* is a river of ice that "flows" down a mountainside. Like a river of running water, it cuts out a stream bed for itself and transports vast amounts of rock and soil from the mountain's top and sides to the valley below.

Glaciers are formed in high places where there is snow all the year round. As fresh snow falls and piles up on the snows of previous winters, the snowfield becomes deeper and heavier until the bottom layers are compressed into a sheet of solid ice.

When this huge mass of snow and ice reaches a certain thickness, it breaks away of its own weight and begins to slide, or "flow," down the mountain. Then new layers of snow and ice collect in the crevice made when the glacier tore itself from the mountain wall.

A glacier flows very slowly, usually only a few inches a day. It continues downward until its lower edge reaches a point on the mountainside where the temperatures are warm enough to melt snow and ice in summer. There it begins to melt, and the water keeps going on in the form of streams and rivers.

If a glacier ends at the edge of the sea, large chunks of it break off and become icebergs.

What was the ice age?

Thousands of years ago, a series of glaciers spread southward from the North Pole and buried more than one fourth of the earth's land surface under a crushing sheet of ice. The ice covered all of what today is Canada, all of New England and New York, the entire Great Lakes area and many parts of the western plains.

As the great glaciers slowly advanced, they leveled mountains, changed the courses of old rivers and created new ones, gouged out the Great Lakes basin and filled the lakes with water as the ice melted and the glaciers finally receded.

They left behind thousands of new lakes, new hills and valleys, and the rock-strewn landscape of New England which marked their lower edge.

Glaciers are bodies of ice moving down mountains or valleys, forming when snowfalls can't melt fast enough.

Water, Water Everywhere

How are rivers formed?

A heavy rain falls on a hillside, and water drips from the leaves of the trees to the ground. There it collects into little rills, or streams, that cascade down the slope. As these tiny streams follow the contour, or outlinc, of the hill, a number of them merge together to form a larger one. Then this too merges with other flows and at last, all together, they become a small brook.

By the time the water reaches the valley that lies between the hills, hundreds, perhaps thousands, of these little rills and rivulets have flowed together to make a broad river. And now the current slows down, and the river becomes more leisurely and unhurried.

Ever since the water started running down from the hilltop, it has been carrying pebbles and bits of soil along with it. Now, as the river slows down, it may

A river is seen winding down from the mountains.

The heat in the earth from the sun rises at night.

As the sun rises, the soil and the air begin to heat up.

leave some of the heavier part of its load along the way. These deposits of stones and silt often create an obstruction in the river bed that causes the current to swerve to the opposite bank, which it then tends to scoop out.

In turn, this scooped-out bank sends the current back to the opposite side again. And the result is a series of curves that make the river wind from side to side like a giant snake.

The sun's heat evaporates water and forms clouds.

Sometimes rainfalls may be so unusually heavy that the normal river banks cannot contain them. Then the rivers overflow into the surrounding land and cause a flood.

What causes floods?

Floods can be terribly destructive. They often wash away fertile topsoil and may leave the land unfit for cultivation for years to follow. They are dread destroyers of property, sometimes washing away entire towns and taking a horrible toll of human lives.

However, some floods have good results instead of bad. Such an overflowing of water is the annual flooding of the Nile River in Egypt.

Each spring, as regular as clockwork, the heavy rains of central Africa pour into the headwaters of the Nile and cause it to overflow the banks of its lower valley. This great volume of water spreads out over the desert and leaves behind it a rich deposit of soil that has been washed down from the mountains of the interior.

In this fertile coating of soil, the Egyptians grow their crops of cotton, fruit and grain. Then, after a year has passed — after the crops have been harvested and the land has again been baked dry by the torrid desert sun — the floods return to make the earth rich and fertile once more.

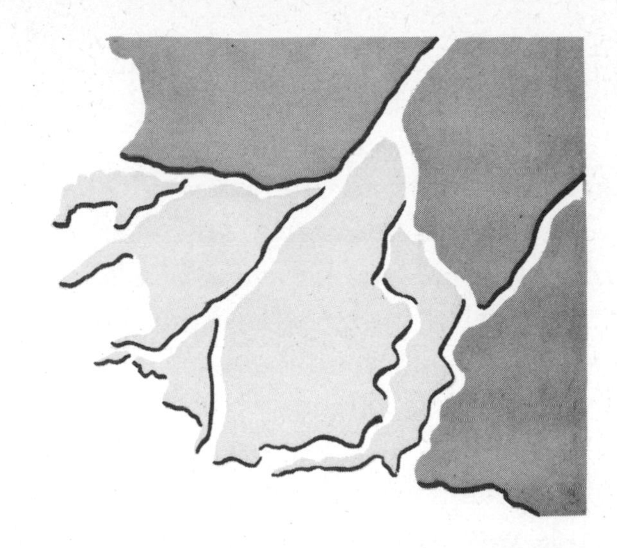

Diagram of very fertile land known as a river delta

A great river like the Mississippi pours billions of gallons of water a day back into the sea. This water contains millions of tons of mud and silt and rock fragments which the river has been carrying down out of the land through which it has flowed.

What is a delta?

As the swift currents of the river hit

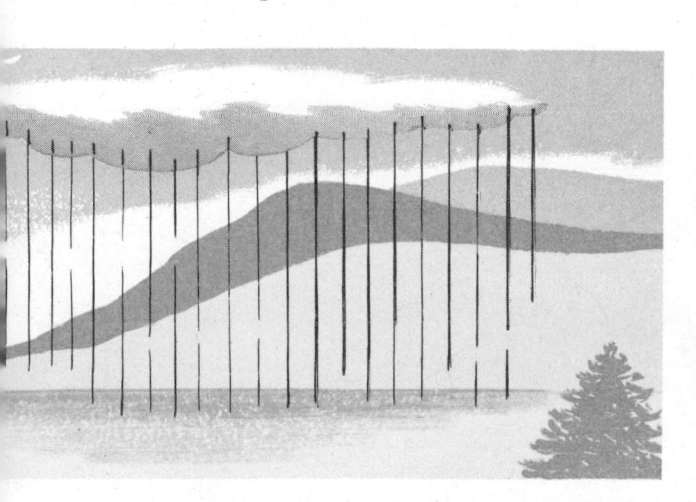

If cloud is blown to cool place: rain falls; to warm place: moisture is absorbed and cloud disappears.

the heavier, quieter waters of the sea, they are quickly slowed down. As a result, immense quantities of this mud and silt settle to the bottom at the river's mouth to create a wide, flat area of very fertile land known as a *delta*.

The deltas of the Mississippi and the Nile, particularly, are known for the extremely rich farmlands which they have built up over the centuries. And most of the country which is now the Netherlands was built up from deltas of the Rhine and other rivers which flowed from the German highlands down to the North Sea.

What causes fresh- and salt-water lakes?

All of the water in the world moves in a continuous cycle. The sun evaporates it from the surface of the sea. There it condenses and falls back to the earth as rain. And the rainwater flows through rivers back to the sea again.

Some of this water, however, is detoured on its journey and trapped for a time in lakes.

Lakes are fed by rivers, and also drained by them. Where this two-way system of in-take and out-go is working, the water of the lake is as sweet as that of the rivers, and is known as a fresh-water lake. But where there is no outlet from the lake, the water becomes salty.

The Caspian Sea in Asia Minor, the largest lake in the world, is a salt-water lake. So are the Dead Sea in the Middle East and the Great Salt Lake in Utah. The largest fresh-water lake is Lake Superior, on the United States-Canadian border. It is 350 miles long and 160 miles wide. Second in size is Lake Victoria in Africa.

Why do lakes and swamps dry up?

Lakes, as a whole, are the least permanent of the earth's geographic features. Even at the moment they are born, they begin to dry up. All lakes, even the largest ones, are in this continuous drying-up process. Lake Superior, for example, is only a remnant of a once much larger lake that was formed by a glacier.

The Everglades: A great tract of Florida swamp land.

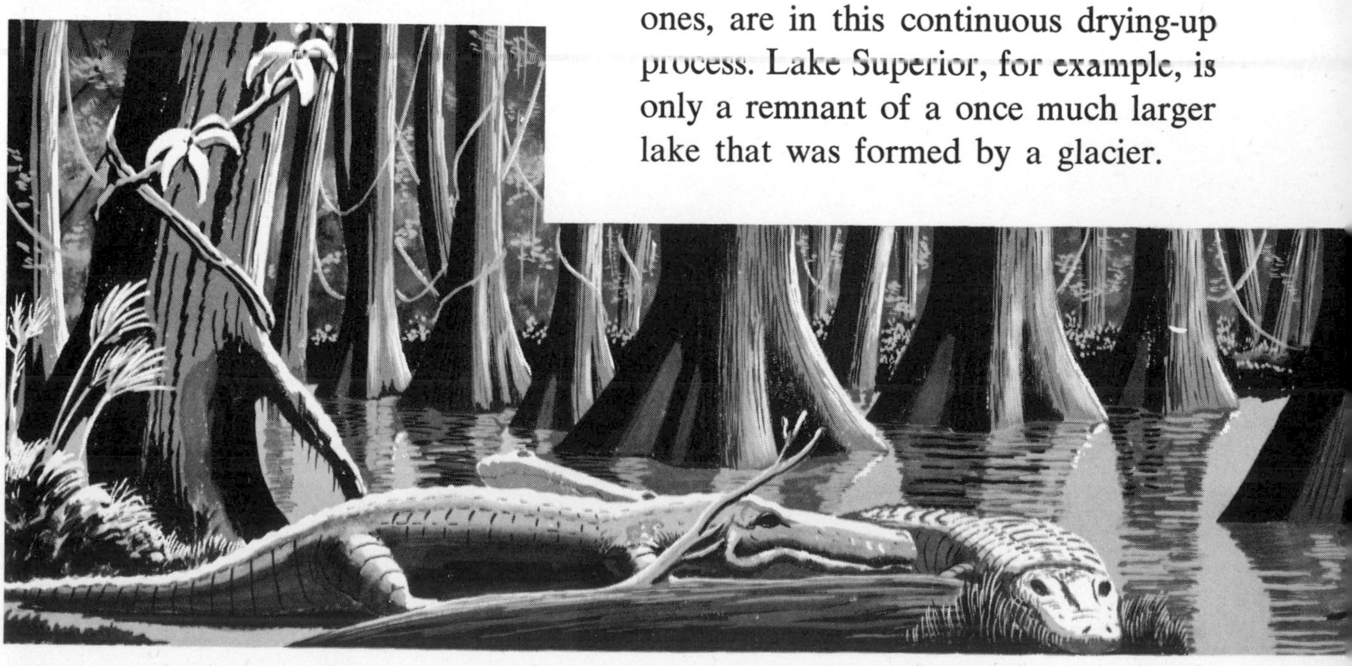

Strangely enough, the rivers that feed lakes and fill them up are also the means of eventually destroying them. As soon as a lake basin is formed, the feeding rivers begin to deposit large quantities of silt and sediment on the lake bottom. Over a long enough period of time, these deposits fill the lake bed completely, turning it first into a swamp and then a meadow. Finally, the last of the water runs off in rivers and continues on its interrupted journey to the sea.

The greatest expanse of swampland in the world, the Florida Everglades, is the remaining part of what was once the ocean floor. The land rose up, and the line of the sea retreated, but not far enough to dry up the area completely.

However, the Everglades are gradually going dry. Parts of them have been drained artificially to create farmlands and townsites, but by doing this, man has only helped to speed up Nature's process. Streams have already begun to take form in the 'Glades, and in time they will serve the same purpose as the man-made drainage ditches. Then, on some distant day, the entire area of the Everglades will be rich, fertile farming and ranching country.

What is quicksand?

Quicksand is a very loose, very light kind of sand which is mixed with water. It is usually found in swamps and other wet places on top of a heavy clay base through which the water cannot drain off.

Quicksand looks like ordinary sand, which is why unlucky animals, and sometimes people, stumble into it by mistake and sink. Unlike grains of ordinary sand, which have angular edges, quicksand grains are round. The underlying water separates them and lifts them up — in a sense, it "floats" them — and thus the sand cannot sustain solid weight. Any heavy object that falls into quicksand sinks as though through water, but much more slowly.

How does water get under the ground?

Every time it rains, a certain amount of rain water is soaked up by the earth. Some of it is held by the soil, and feeds the roots of growing plants. But most of it seeps on down to a level where all the cracks and openings in the underlying rocks are completely filled with water.

Indeed, there is more water under the ground than there is in all the surface lakes and pools.

As a rule, the level of this underground water tends to follow the contours of the earth's surface. For this reason it is possible to get water from a well drilled on top of a hill as well as from one drilled in the valley below.

When the level of this underground water comes into contact with the sur-

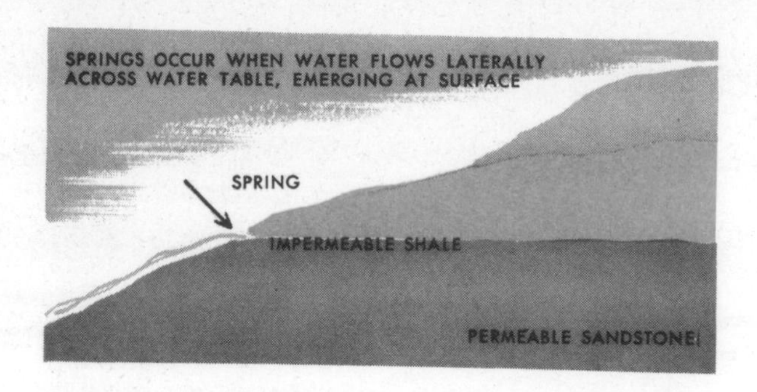

face — usually on the side of a hill — the water seeps out to create a spring. This spring water is cooler and usually tastes sweeter than river water because it has not been exposed to the heat of the sun.

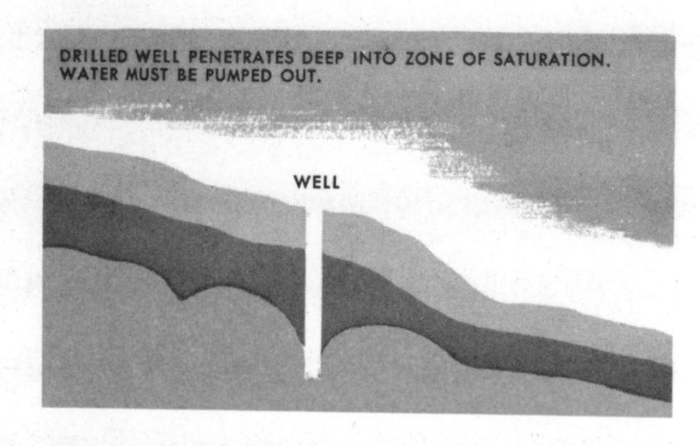

What is an artesian flow?

Sometimes a layer of water-bearing rock is encased by strata of solid rock on top as well as underneath. This, then, becomes a sort of natural "water pipe" from which the water inside cannot escape. This water-bearing strata is called an *artesian* (ar-TEE-zhan) *flow*.

If a well is drilled down to tap this imprisoned water supply, the pressure from either side will force the water to the surface. If there is a natural crack in the earth, and if the pressure is great enough, the water will gush up like a natural fountain.

Often the water in artesian streams flows hundreds of miles, from the place

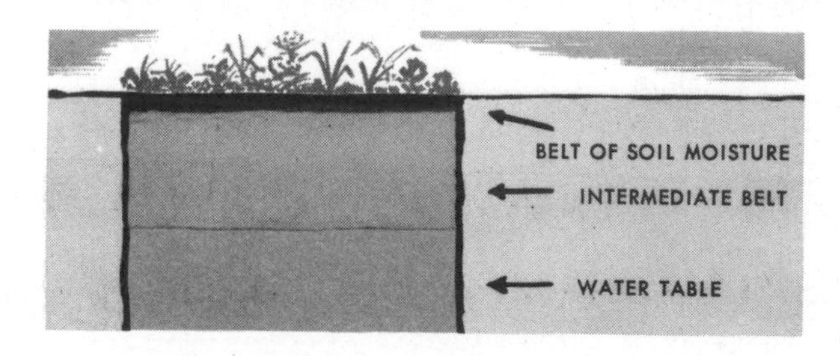

where it descended into the earth as rain to the point where it emerges again from wells. For this reason — since they are not dependent upon local conditions of rainfall — artesian wells usually supply an endless source of water, even in times of extreme drought, when other wells in the vicinity go dry.

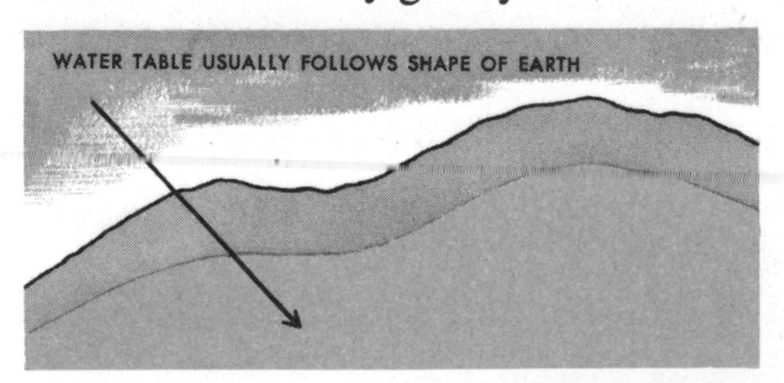

What is connate water?

Most underground water, as we have seen, comes from rain that seeps into the earth. But there is still another kind, called *connate* water, that has lain sealed up in pockets of rock deep within the earth for many millions of years.

When the sedimentary rock formations were first formed on the bottoms of the ancient seas, a certain amount of sea water was trapped inside of them. Then, when the sea floors rose up and became part of the land, the trapped water deposits rose with them.

A common example of connate water is the salt water that is often brought up from oil wells.

A diagram of a connate, or trapped, water deposit

The Earth's Surface

What is a desert like?

When we look out over the dry, waterless desert, it seems to be without life. Except for a few shriveled scrub bushes and cactus spines, there is almost no vegetation to cover the sandy, rocky ground. In places, the fierce, dry wind has blown the rocks bare of sand and soil, and has cut the rocks themselves into weird, twisted patterns.

By day, the hot, fiery ball of the sun beats down out of the clear, cloudless sky so blazingly that a man could not live for more than an hour or two without some kind of shade. Then, when the sun sinks at last behind the desert's rim, the temperature may drop so sharply that an unprotected traveler is in danger of freezing.

It rarely rains in the desert, and when it does, the rainfall is usually scanty. But on rare occasions a cloudburst floods down without warning from the sky. When this happens, the desert plants greedily drink up the moisture and store it in their long roots, so that it will continue to nourish them during the long, hot dry spell that is sure to follow.

Dunes are sand piles swept together by the wind.

The seeds of the desert plants lie dormant in the dry earth for months, and even years, at a time. Then the magic of the rain touches them and overnight they burst into glorious life, briefly covering the entire desert with a brilliant coat of many colors. Then, just as quickly as they bloomed, they wither and die, waiting, it would seem, for the next rain to bring them back to life again.

How can wind and rain carve rocks?

We know that wind and water are constantly at work reshaping the surface of the earth. Perhaps the most unusual examples of this erosive action can be found in the deserts of our American West.

The strange rock formations pictured here are in Bryce Canyon National Park, in Utah.

The action of water over a period of millions of years eroded the plain that is today Bryce Canyon. Pinnacles of amazing shapes and colors have made the canyon a national monument. Insert (left) is a natural bridge.

At one time, this was a broad, sandy plain. But as millions of years went by, the rivers that flowed across it dissolved the limestone in the underlying rock and ate away the harder rocks bit by tiny bit — until, at last, Bryce Canyon became the place of fairyland palaces and monuments that it is today.

The action of the wind is nearly as important in the reshaping of the land as that of water.

In desert regions, the wind blows away the sand and shifts it from place to place, often leaving outcroppings of bare rock. Then the wind-blown sand is blasted against the rock with the same effect that sandpaper has when you rub it across a piece of wood. Gradually the rock is worn away — the softer parts going first and the harder parts remaining. The results are often such odd and beautiful pieces of wind-

and-sand sculpture as natural rock bridges or balanced rocks that look like giant tops.

How has man helped to change the surface of the earth?

We have seen that the forces of nature are constantly at work changing the surface of the earth. Man has also done his share to alter the appearance and characteristics of parts of the land. Sometimes, as in the instance of the famous area of the Southwest which was appropriately called the Dust Bowl, this has had very tragic effects.

At one time, this part of Texas and Oklahoma was a lush grassland. The thick grass roots held in the moisture of the soil, and even in times of drought the land was green and fertile.

Then farmers began to plow up the grasslands to plant crops. And in the early 1930's, there came a long dry spell. The crops failed, and the loose soil, with no grass roots to hold it together, began to blow away in vast dust storms.

For many years, the land produced no crops, and most of the people who lived in the area left it and moved to other parts of the country.

The use of irrigation ditches in sandy, barren stretches of land has resulted in productive farmland acreage.

Gradually, however, the people who stayed on the land began to plant it again with grass. And the farmers learned how to plant their crops in such a way that the soil could be conserved. Today, what was once the Dust Bowl is again prosperous farming and grazing land.

How can a desert be made to bloom?

Sometimes, unlike what happened in the Dust Bowl, man has often changed the face of the land for the better. When the first settlers went west, parts of California and other states were dry, arid deserts where nothing could grow but cactus and other desert plants useless to man.

By digging irrigation ditches and bringing in water from distant rivers, farmers changed the earth from unproductive desert sand to fertile soil. And today, large areas of what once were deserts, are now the most fruitful farmlands in America.

What rocks make up the earth's surface?

Basically, there are three kinds of rocks that make up the earth's surface.

1. *Igneous* (IG-nee-us), meaning "fire." Igneous rocks are the oldest, since they were formed from the hardening of molten magma when the earth first began to cool and solidify billions of years ago. Thus they were the ancestors of the other two rock types, as well as of all sand and soil.

The two most common and most important igneous rocks are *granite* (GRAN-it) and *basalt* (ba-SALT).

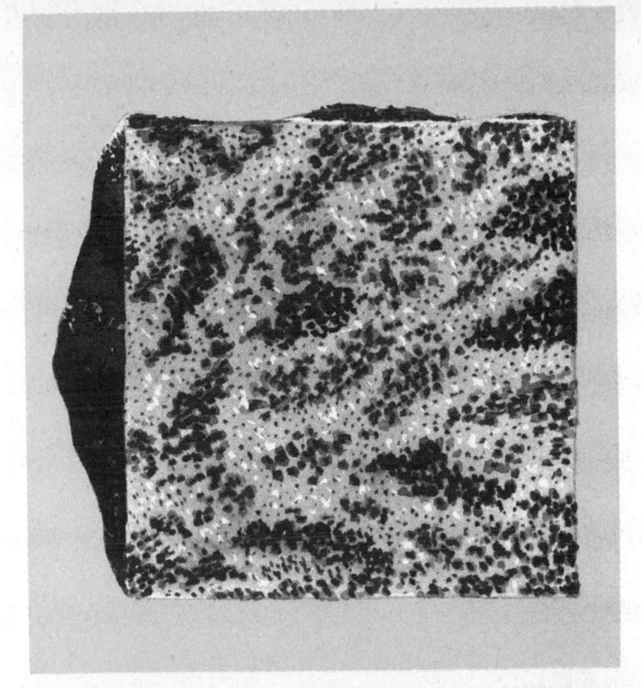

Granite is an igneous rock (formed from fire or heat).

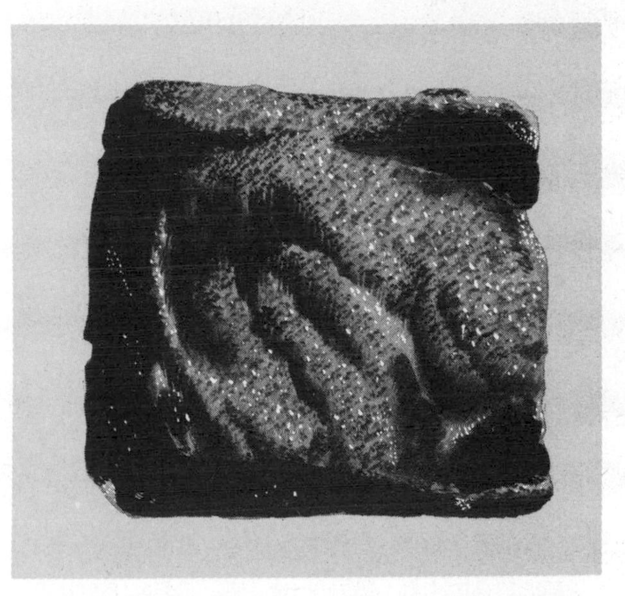

Basalt is another igneous rock of volcanic origin.

Granite, found over most of the United States, is the most widely used building stone because of its strength and endurance. It ranges in color from white to gray to green to pink to red.

Basalt, sometimes called traprock, is the stone that is most usually crushed and used to make surfaces for roads. It varies in color from gray to black.

2. *Sedimentary* (sed-ih-MEN-tary), meaning "a settling." Sedimentary

rocks are composed of what at one time, many millions of years ago, were layers of sand, gravel, mud and sediment lying on the bottoms of ancient seas. These materials were hardened into true rock by the great pressures that were exerted upon them.

The most common sedimentary rocks are sandstone, limestone and shale.

3. *Metamorphic* (met-a-MORE-fik), meaning "made over." Metamorphic rocks are those which at one time were either igneous or sedimentary, but which were changed into a different form by forces such as heat and pressure which came from deep within the earth.

The metamorphic rocks we most frequently see are marble, slate and quartzite.

Marble, one of the hardest of all stones, was "made over" from limestone, one of the softest. It is widely used for monuments and building.

Slate was "made over" from layers of compressed shale and clay. This strange rock splits easily into thin, uniform sheets with a smooth, straight surface. It is commonly used as roofing material for houses.

Quartzite (KWORTS-ite) looks a great deal like sandstone, from which it was "made over." But while sandstone is relatively soft, quartzite is among the hardest of rocks. An outcropping of quartzite often takes the form of a cliff, from which the softer rocks have been eroded away.

Here are some unusual kinds of rocks.

Asbestos is found in metamorphic rocks in the form of long silky fibers. These fibers can be woven into a fireproof cloth that is used to make brake linings and fire-fighting clothing.

Flint was used by early primitive man to make his knives and arrowheads.

Pudding stones are odd-looking stones most usually found in the beds of streams. They are a form of sandstone in which small pebbles, rock fragments, fine sand and various other rock-forming minerals have all been mixed up like a pudding and cemented together in a solid mass.

Petrified wood, found in the Petrified Forest of Arizona, is not really a piece of wood that has turned to stone. What actually happened was that millions of years ago, a tree fell into a swamp where the water contained a high proportion of dissolved quartz, one of the rock-forming minerals. The water soaked into the cells of the wood, and as the wood decayed, the quartz hardened to form the same pattern as the fibers of the tree.

What are minerals?

In general, a *mineral* may be defined as any solid element or compound that is made up of chemical substances found in nature.

For example, common table salt — known as halite (HAL-ite) is composed of sodium and chlorine. A diamond is formed from carbon, which is also the basic ingredient of coal. Rubies and sapphires come from corundum (cor-UN-dum) which, in another form, is the rough, black rock that is used to make grindstones.

Rocks

SANDSTONE

SHALE

SLATE

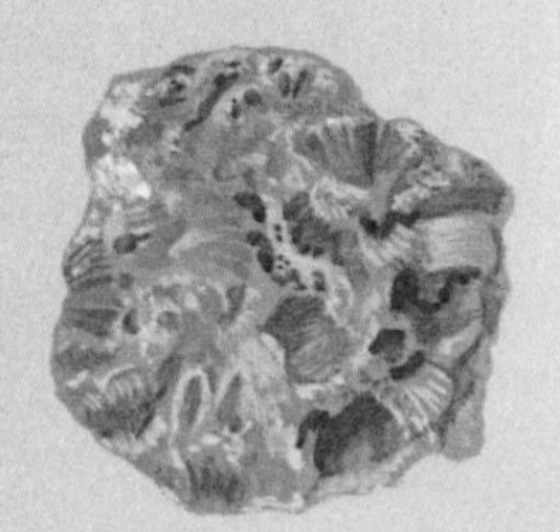
LIMESTONE

MARBLE

QUARTZITE

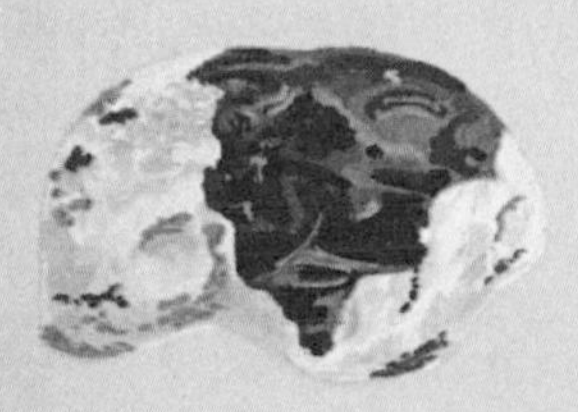
FLINT

PUDDING STONE

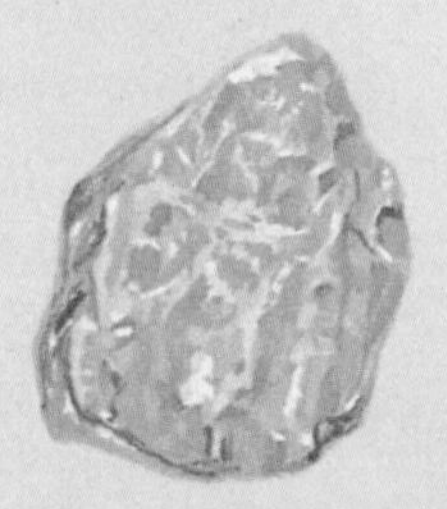
TALC

Minerals

HALITE

CRYSTALS OF SULPHUR

HEMATITE

CORUNDUM CRYSTAL

RHODONITE

FLUORITE

All rocks are made from a great many kinds of minerals, and when you break open a piece of rock, you can see these minerals — like quartz and mica — usually in crystal form.

Here are some common minerals that you might find in rocks around your home.

Quartz is probably the commonest of all mineral crystals. It is found in all sizes — some long and slender, some thick and squat — but all quartz crystals have identically the same shape. They are six-sided prisms, with six-sided pyramids on the top and bottom. Quartz is one of the hardest of all minerals. It cannot be scratched with a knife, but it will scratch or cut glass. Quartz sand is the basic ingredient in glass-making.

Mica (MY-kuh) is found in granite and other igneous rocks. It can be split into paper-thin sheets that are transparent, flexible and fireproof. It is used to make the little windows in electric fuses and the larger windows in oven doors. In some primitive countries, it has been used as window glass.

Talc is a curious white mineral so soft that you can scratch it with your fingernail. It feels greasy to the touch. It is used commercially as a lubricant, and as the base for talcum powder.

Calcite (KAL-site) is a common mineral that is found in a number of forms. It may appear in thin sheets, like mica, or in diamond-shaped crystals, like quartz. You may sometimes find a crystal of calcite that is as transparent as glass, but the curious thing about it is that when you look through it you see everything double. If you break a calcite crystal with a hammer, each tiny fragment will be a perfect little six-sided shape with smooth surfaces and equal angles.

Amber is not a true mineral, since it is the fossilized remains of the resin of ancient fir trees that fell into swamps. But it is an interesting mineral-like substance to examine. Quite often the bodies of insects that were trapped in the resin when it was liquid, thousands of years ago, are still perfectly preserved.

Pyrite (PIE-rite) is known as "fool's gold" because it fooled so many miners in the Old West into thinking that they had found a gold mine. Pyrite, a beautiful, sparkling mineral, is often used to make ornaments and jewelry.

How can you make your own mineral crystals?

Put two or three teaspoonfuls of table salt into half a glass of water. Stir it well. Now suspend a piece of string into the liquid from a stick laid across the rim of the glass. Put it away in a cool place for several days. At the end of that time, the salt will have formed crystals on the end of the string in the shape of little cubes of pure halite that sparkle like a cluster of miniature diamonds.

An ancient forest scene

Treasures in the Ground

How was oil made?

About three hundred million years ago, great forests of tree ferns covered the hot, swampy earth. As they wilted and died, they tumbled into the swamps, and there they sank down into the ooze. As thousands of centuries crept slowly by, the buried tree ferns were covered up by other ferns and trees that fell into the water on top of them.

Then the face of the earth slowly changed, and the swamp was covered over with silt which turned to rock. And at last the land sank down and was swallowed up by the waters of the seas. More millions of years passed, and the land rose up from the sea bottoms again to form hills and plains and plateaus. And what had once been the tree-filled swamps were now imprisoned between thick layers of rock thousands of feet below the surface.

But while all this land-change had been going on, a curious thing had been happening. Pressures from inside the earth had brought about a chemical change in the masses of trees and ferns and other vegetable matter that had sunk into the original swamps so many millions of years before. Now it had been changed into an underground reservoir of the thick black liquid which we call petroleum, or crude oil.

Sometimes these underground deposits came close enough to the surface so that the oil seeped up and formed black, sticky puddles. And the ancient people used this crude oil for lights and cooking fires.

It was not until about a hundred years ago, that scientists learned to drill for petroleum and refine it into such products as gasoline, kerosene and lubricating oil. But in the modern world, it has become our most important fuel. Without it, we could not operate our automobiles or ships or factories or power plants.

Oil deposits are usually trapped under the ground between layers of folded rock. The petroleum floats on a pool of connate water, with a pocket of natural gas on top. When a well is drilled down to the oil deposit, the pressure of the gases forces the petroleum to the surface.

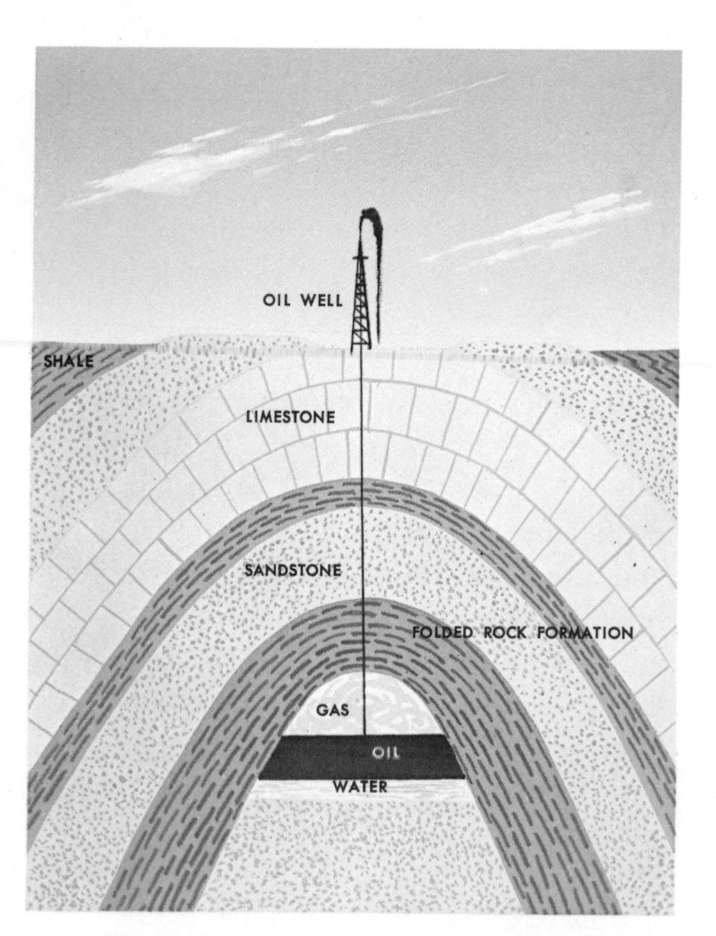

This is a cutaway view of an oil deposit in the earth.

This is a fossil leaf which has been embedded in coal.

How was coal made?

Coal was formed in much the same way as oil, and at about the same time in the earth's geological history. Vast masses of vegetable matter fell into ancient swamps, rotted, were covered up by mud and silt which turned into stone, sank into the sea and then rose up again.

But in some strange way, these rotted tree ferns and mosses, instead of changing into liquid oil, had been subjected to different kinds of forces which transformed them into the hard, black, brittle rock which we call coal.

Coal lies under the ground in long, thick seams, sandwiched in between layers of slate or shale. Sometimes, when a piece of coal is broken open, the fossil imprint of a fern leaf can be clearly seen, still as perfectly shaped as when it grew upon the ancient tree.

Why are iron and steel important?

Iron is perhaps the world's most important mineral. From iron we make steel, and from steel we make most of the necessary things that we use every day — buildings, automobiles, ships, trains, tools, machinery, stoves, furnaces, refrigerators. A day never passes during which we do not depend upon some article made of iron or steel.

Although iron was one of the most abundant elements from which our earth was made — and though the earth's central core is almost pure iron — iron practically never occurs in its pure state on the surface where man can get at it. Instead, iron is mixed with other minerals in the form of *ore,* and the ore itself is imbedded in the rock of the crust. Extracting it is a long and difficult process.

The most important deposits of iron ore in the United States are around Lake Superior. Here the ore lies near to the surface, and it is scraped out of great open pits by steam shovels. The ore is then shipped in cargo vessels through the Great Lakes to the mills of Ohio and Pennsylvania where it is converted into steel.

How are other metals useful to us?

Next to iron, copper is our most useful metal. It is essential to the manufacture of electrical equipment, and has many other uses as well. Combined with zinc,

Bessemer converters shown in operation in a steel mill. In the process, steel is manufactured from cast iron.

Bauxite, from which aluminum comes, is mined here in open-pit fashion. Arkansas leads in its production.

it becomes brass; and when tin is added, it becomes bronze.

There is even more aluminum than iron in the great mass of minerals that make up the earth's crust. But most of this metal is tightly imprisoned inside certain rocks, and there is no practical method by which it can be extracted.

However, under certain conditions, these rocks have weathered and broken down into a claylike mineral called *bauxite* (BAWK-site). And it is from this bauxite clay that we get all of the aluminum which we use in industry.

Aluminum is a very light, very strong metal. It is used where lightness is as important as strength, such as in the manufacture of airplane bodies and motors, household furniture and kitchen appliances, scientific instruments and certain kinds of machinery.

There are a great many other metals that play an important part in our daily lives.

Tin is chiefly used to put a protective coating over steel so that the food in "tin cans" will not spoil.

Chromium (CRO-mee-um) is mixed with steel to produce the alloy called "stainless steel," which is used for automobile trimming and other products that require extreme hardness, plus resistance to rust.

Gold, which we consider to be the

"most precious" metal, is used for money and jewelry, but has little use in industry.

Silver is also used for jewelry, and for fine tableware. It is the best known conductor of electricity, and is therefore used in the very finest electrical equipment.

Uranium (u-RAY-nee-um), the "miracle metal" of modern times, is our chief source of atomic power. It is found in many kinds of rocks, such as uranite, carnotite, davidite and gummite.

What are the "precious" minerals?

Since earliest times, people all over the world have treasured rare and beautiful mineral stones as their most prized possessions. The most precious of these gem stones are diamonds, emeralds, rubies and sapphires.

Diamonds are the hardest of all stones. A diamond will cut any other known substance, but the only thing that will cut a diamond is another diamond. Most diamonds come from Africa, but they are found all over the world. There are diamond mines in India, South America and the United States. The largest diamond ever found, the Cullinan, was discovered by a farmer in South Africa who happened to see a shiny stone sticking out of the ground. It was about the size of a man's fist and was cut up to become part of the British Crown Jewels.

Emeralds, if they are large and have no flaws, are worth more than diamonds. Most of them come from Ecuador, Peru and Colombia in South America. True emeralds are a deep green in color.

Rubies, at least the finest ones, come from Burma. The most valuable of these fiery red stones are known as "pigeon blood" rubies, since from ancient times the standard of perfection has been to compare the color of the stone to that of a drop of blood from a freshly killed pigeon.

Sapphires are found in many hues and colors, but the most valuable are those of a deep cornflower blue which seem to glow with an inner light that takes the form of a star. These are known as "star sapphires."

What are some common gem stones?

In addition to the really precious gems, there are a great many beautiful gem stones that any boy or girl might find not far from home. Some of these are:

Aquamarine, a lovely bluish-green stone that is usually found embedded in rock ledges.

Amethyst, a delicate purple stone found over most of the United States, ordinarily in clusters of small crystals.

Agate, a form of quartz that has concentric (circles one within another) layers of different colors. When cut and polished, agate makes jewelry of gleaming beauty.

Clear Quartz. Sometimes one is lucky enough to find a quartz crystal with a hollow cavity inside that contains a drop or two of water. This water somehow became imprisoned inside the stone when the crystal was formed, and since it cannot evaporate, it will remain there forever.

Gem Stones

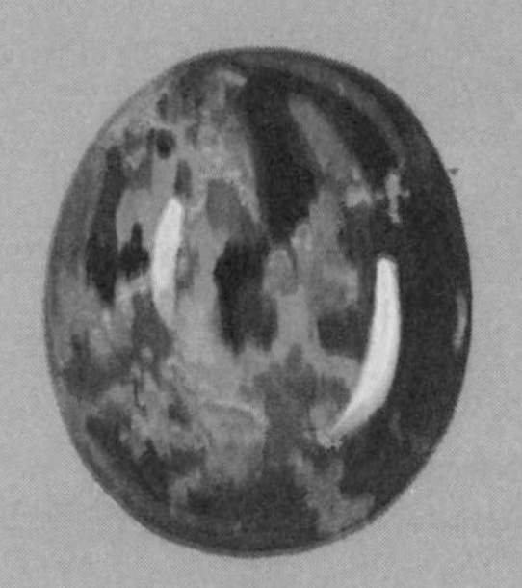

OPAL

EMERALD

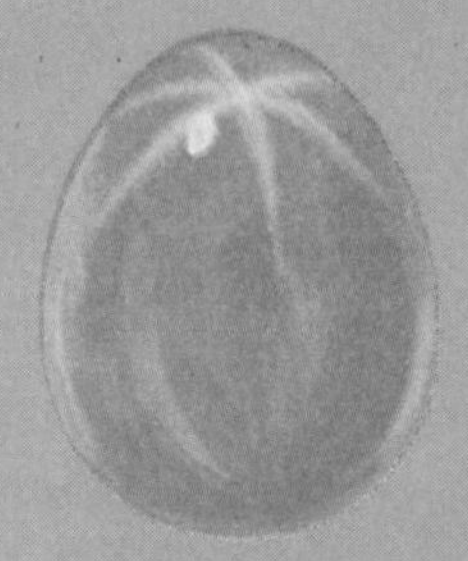

STAR SAPPHIRE

ALEXANDRITE

DIAMOND

AQUAMARINE

TOURMALINE

RUBY

GREEN PERIDOT

TOPAZ

JADE

CARNELIAN

MOSS AGATE

STEATITE

LAPIS LAZULI

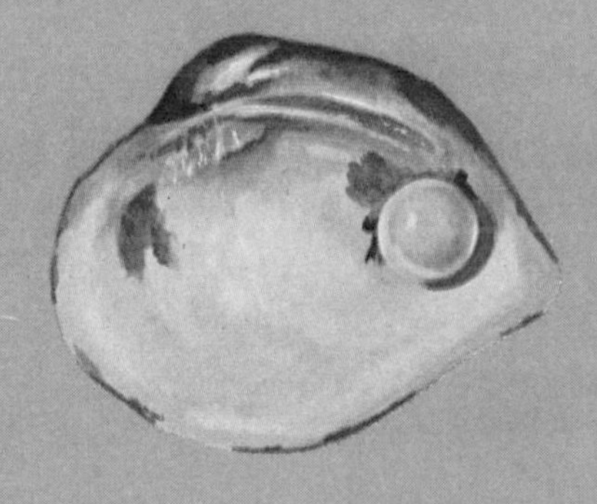

PEARL

AMETHYST

BERYL

MALACHITE

TURQUOISE

ONYX

CHRYSOBERYL

Chalcedony, the smooth, round, semi-transparent pebbles that are often found on beaches or along the banks of streams.

Garnet, a stone that is abundant all over the United States. Most are brownish in color, but the most prized stones are deep, clear red or emerald green.

Sun Stone. Tiny specks of mica imbedded in clear quartz crystal give this unusual stone the appearance of flashing sparks of fire from deep inside.

The Underground Rooms

Of what is the soil made?

The thin layer of soil that covers most of the surface of the earth nourishes all of the life that exists on land. Without it, no grass or grain or vegetables could grow to furnish food for animals and men.

Soil is a combination of decaying rock and decaying vegetable matter. The hot summer sun heats bare rock and expands and cracks it. The ice and snow of winter contracts and splits it. Rain washes tiny grains of the weathered rock into small depressions of the ground. Here the rock particles mingle with dead leaves and decaying plants — and the two form the carpet of soil that covers the earth's floor.

You can prove this by dropping a handful of soil from a garden into a glass of water. Stir it up, and then allow it to settle. Some particles will float to the top. The rest will sink to the bottom. If you examine the floating particles, you will see that they are small bits and pieces of leaves and roots and other vegetable matter. The particles that sink are bits of sand and gravel, remnants of the weathered and broken-up rock.

During most of the earth's lifetime, it had no soil. There was nothing on the face of the land but barren rock. Then tiny plants from the sea water, called lichens, began to grow on rocks at the ocean's edge. Their little roots penetrated the rocks' surface and caused bits of it to scale off. Then, as the lichens died and decayed, they mingled with the rock dust and gradually began to turn into soil.

More plants grew, and they in turn became part of the soil. And in this way the carpet of soil began creeping inland from the seashores until it had covered most of the earth's land.

The soil is divided into three layers.

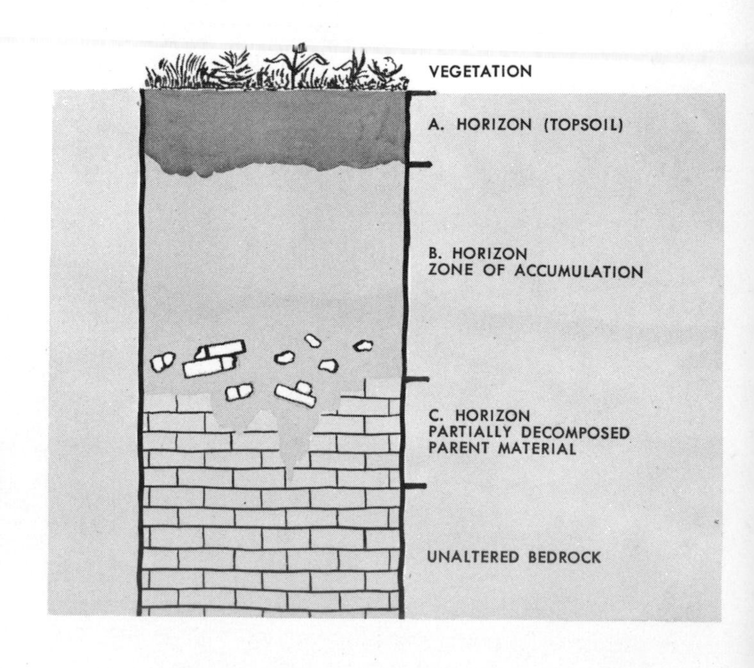

This interior of a cave shows stalactites extending from the ceiling and stalagmites rising from the floor.

The bottom layer is solid bedrock, with its upper edges slowly decomposing, or decaying, and flaking off.

The middle layer is hard-packed, and contains rock fragments and pebbles mixed with clay and heavy earth. Minerals seep down into it from the surface, and up from the ground-water that lies underneath. Only the roots of trees and larger plants penetrate this middle layer.

The top layer is the part of the soil in which we plant things. It is soft and crumbly, and is composed sometimes almost entirely of decayed vegetable matter. This layer extends down for only a few inches.

And yet, in this thin layer of topsoil, an amazing amount of plant and animal life is present.

How were caves formed?

A cave is the nearest thing in Nature to a fairyland world. Fantastic icicles of stone hang from the roof of a cave in a million shapes and sizes. Tapering stonc spires rise up from the floor and stone flowers, with delicately colored petals, grow in cracks between the rocks.

Caves are usually found in those parts of the world where the underlying rock is limestone. The chief part of limestone is the mineral *calcite,* and this is readily dissolved by the small amount of *carbonic acid* that is present in most surface water.

A cave has its beginning when rainwater seeps into the ground and flows between layers of limestone. As the water passes, it dissolves tiny parts of the stone and carries the dissolved material along with it. This ceaseless weathering of the rock by the water continues for countless thousands of years. The pathways that the water has cut out for itself are enlarged, until at last the underlying rock is filled with passageways that wind and twist down through the rock layers, and sometimes widen and spread out to form huge underground rooms.

What are stalactites and stalagmites?

When ground water seeps down through the earth, it reacts upon the limestone over which it passes to form a mineral called *calcium bicarbonate*. As this water slowly filters through the ceiling of the cave, drop by single drop, each drop clings to the ceiling for a moment or so before it drips to the floor. But in that short moment, a slight amount of evaporation takes place, and when the drop of water falls, it leaves behind a tiny amount of calcium bicarbonate.

After many centuries, these tiny deposits build on each other and eventually form a stone "icicle" that hangs down from the ceiling. This is called a *stalactite* (stal-ACK-tite).

When each drop of water falls to the floor beneath the stalactite, it splashes and leaves another small deposit of calcium bicarbonate. These deposits gradually build upward, and form a stone pillar rising up from the floor, which is called a *stalagmite* (stal-AG-mite).

In the course of a long time, the stalactite hanging down may unite with the stalagmite protruding upward to form a *column*. Sometimes a number of these columns join together and divide the cave into rooms.

Still another kind of mineral "growth" found in caves are the beautiful and delicate clusters of *helictites* (hel-ICK-tites). These are formed, like stalactites, by the gradual evaporation of water. But no one knows quite how they achieved their fantastic shapes.

What are wind caves?

The most common type of shallow caves are formed on the sides of hills or rocky cliffs by the action of the wind. This happens when a layer of soft rock, such as shale, is sandwiched in between two layers of hard sandstone. Wind currents swirl across the face of the hillside and scoop out particles of the shale, often digging quite far back into the mountain.

These are the caves most often used by ancient cave men for their homes, and by wild animals for their lairs.

Often the rolling waters at the base of a waterfall dig out a cave under the overhanging rock. The most famous of these waterfall caves is known as the Cave of the Winds, beneath Niagara

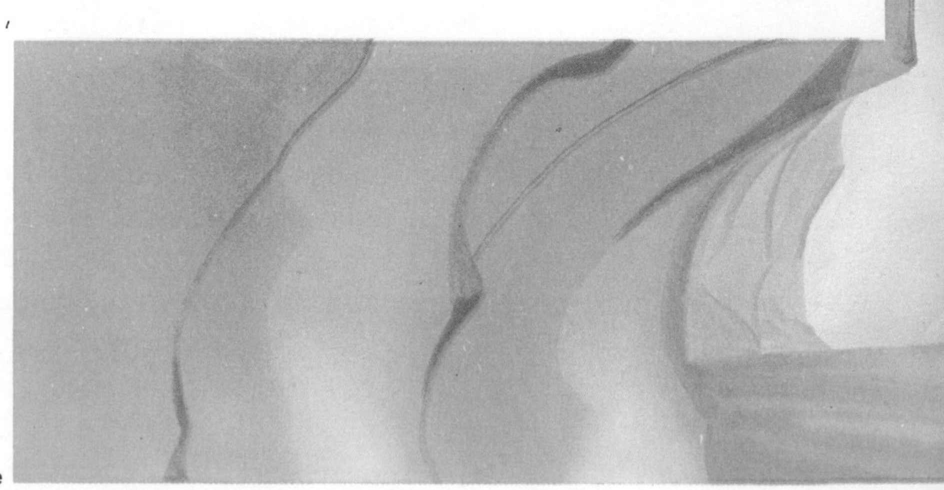

Interior view of an ice cave

Falls. Visitors are taken into it, and there they can stand behind the huge pounding wall of water that roars down from the river above.

What are ice caves?

Some of the most fantastic caves in the world are the ice caves of the European mountains. Ages ago, when the earth's climate was much warmer than it is now, underground rivers tunneled their way through the solid mountain rock. Then the long ice age descended on the Northern Hemisphere, and these rivers froze in their underground beds. Today, they exist as caves of ice.

In places, far under the mountain tops, these ice rivers flow into ice lakes that are as smooth as skating rinks. Sometimes they drop suddenly over a precipice to create solid waterfalls of ice that are nearly half as high as Niagara Falls.

In the open corridors of the caves, columns of ice rise up from the floor like crystal stalagmites. These were created by the slow dripping and re-freezing of melted ice falling from above. Now and then these columns fuse together to form delicately sculptured ice curtains.

Often stalactites of ice hang suspended from the ceiling, so crystal clear that they can act as a gigantic magnifying glass. Occasionally, bubbles of air, imprisoned in a stalactite when it froze, give the huge formation the quality of a gleaming jewel.

Since limestone caves were created by the action of underground water, it is not surprising that many such caves are completely flooded. One of the most amazing of these underwater caverns is Wakulla Cave in Florida.

What are underwater caves?

Wakulla Spring, source of the Wakulla River, is a small lake that is fed entirely by underground water. For many years, scientists had wondered about the source of this water. And so a group of geologists, equipped with skin-diving gear and other equipment, set out to explore it.

They found that underneath the surface of the spring, the cave slanted sharply downward to a depth of nearly 200 feet, and there it began to level off. Its width varied from 70 to 150 feet — and its height, from floor to ceiling, was in places only 5 feet and in others more than 100. The floor was of sand, with patches of clay and limestone rubble.

The divers explored the cavern for a distance of 1,100 feet from the entrance. Here the bottom dropped down sharply into a much wider and deeper section of the cave, but beyond this point the divers could not go without running short of air.

It is believed, however, that Wakulla Cave may extend for several miles to the source of its water supply.

The Beginning of Man

It is only natural that early man should have lived in caves. He had neither the tools nor the skills to build houses — and hillside caves provided ready-made shelters from cold, snow, rain and wild beasts.

What were the cave men like?

As nearly as we can determine, man has been living on the earth for about half a million years. Evidence recently dug up in caves has definitely traced his history back to about 100,000 B.C.

One hundred thousand years ago, man didn't look very much as he does today. He was generally short and squat, with stubby legs and long, thick arms. Most of his body was covered by a heavy mat of hair. His only tools were hatchets and knives made of flint, and he was just learning to use fire to warm his cave home. He was also just learning to speak.

A few years ago, a team of American scientists found a cave in the mountains of Iraq that contained a continuous history of human progress from the Stone Age to the present day. This was Shanidar Cave.

How did we learn about the cave men?

Shanidar is inhabited today by a tribe of Kurdish peasants, but the amazing thing about this cave is that it has

Early man lived in warm and protective caves.

been lived in by humans for about one hundred thousand years!

Luckily for the scientists, the tenants of the cave, from earliest times, were very untidy housekeepers. Instead of sweeping out their trash and refuse, they simply buried it under succeeding layers of dust and dirt. So by digging down into the floor of the cave, the researchers were able to lay bare a cross section of human history — in much the same way that the fossils in layers of sedimentary rocks give us a picture-history of the earth itself.

There were four main layers of packed-down dirt and debris under the cave floor, each one representing a definite period in the history of man's progress.

The top layer dates from the present time to about seven thousand years ago. Here were found pieces of pottery, stones for grinding grain, and the bones of domestic animals—evidences that man was learning to grow his own crops and tend his own herds.

Below this was a layer said to be some twelve thousand years old. There was no indication here that the people of this period knew anything about farming or the care of animals.

The third layer went back in time to about 40,000 B.C. Yet in all of the thirty thousand years that had passed between the laying down of this layer and the one above it, there was no evidence that man had made much progress in his way of living.

Finally, the fourth and last layer of the debris on the floor of Shanidar Cave takes the history of mankind back to its earliest beginnings, about one hundred thousand years ago.

It is from such bits and pieces of evidence as this that we are able to put together a picture of the life of primitive man at the dawn of human time.

Who made the cave paintings?

One day, about a hundred years ago, a little girl and her father were exploring a cave in Spain. As the father was examining ancient flint hammers and arrowheads which he found on the cave floor, the child wandered off into another room carrying a candle to light her way.

Suddenly she looked up to the ceiling of the cave and screamed:

"Bulls! Daddy! Bulls! Come quick!"

Her father came running, and when he reached her, he saw an amazing sight.

There on the ceiling and walls of the cave were the pictures of animals.

Who painted them? Why did the primitive artist paint them in a cave? How did he get light to see by?

Nobody yet knows the answers. All that we know for sure is that the paintings were done by an unknown Stone Age genius about twenty-five thousand years ago.

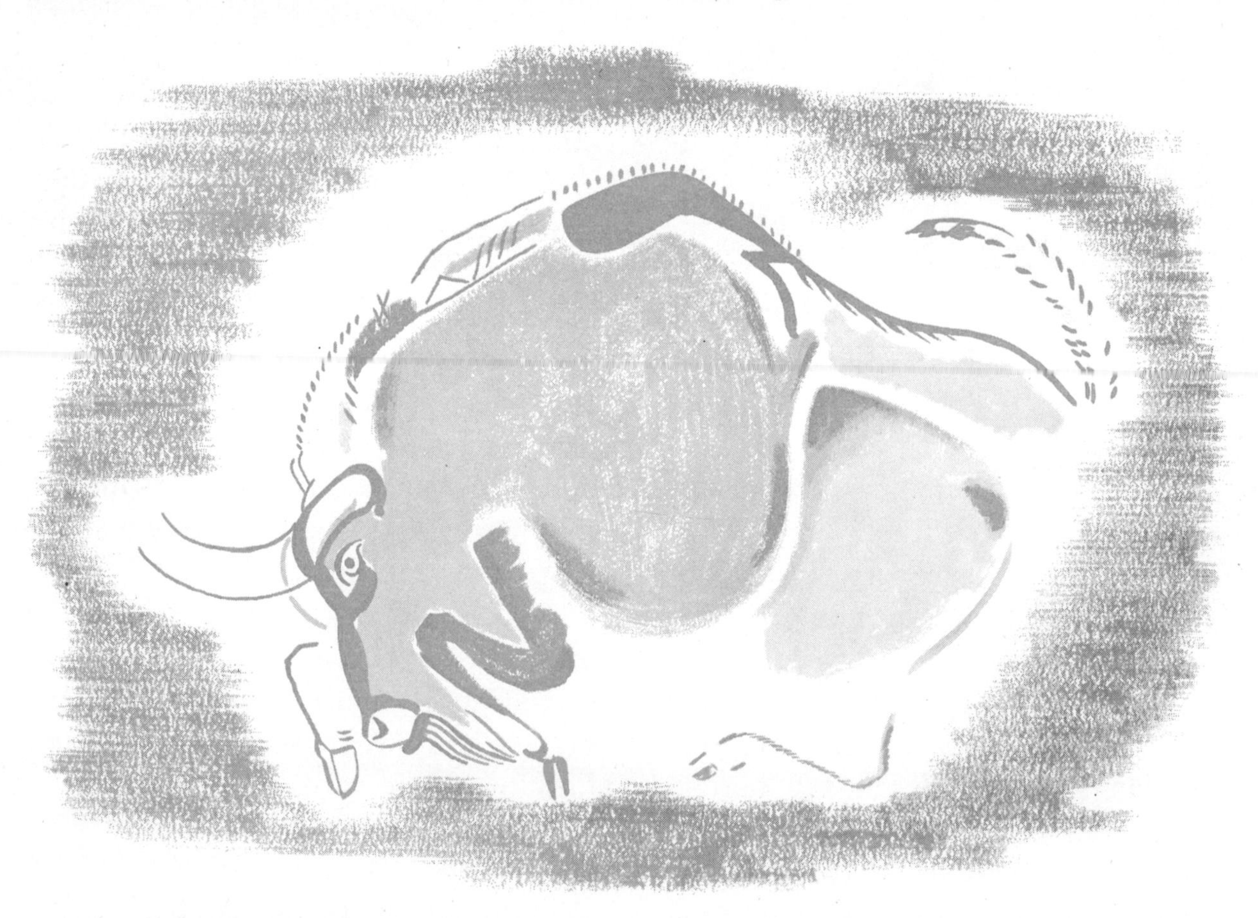

An unknown Stone Age artist drew this picture of a bison on a cave wall in Spain thousands of years ago.

THE HOW AND WHY WONDER BOOK OF ROCKS AND MINERALS

By Nelson W. Hyler
Illustrated by Kenyon Shannon

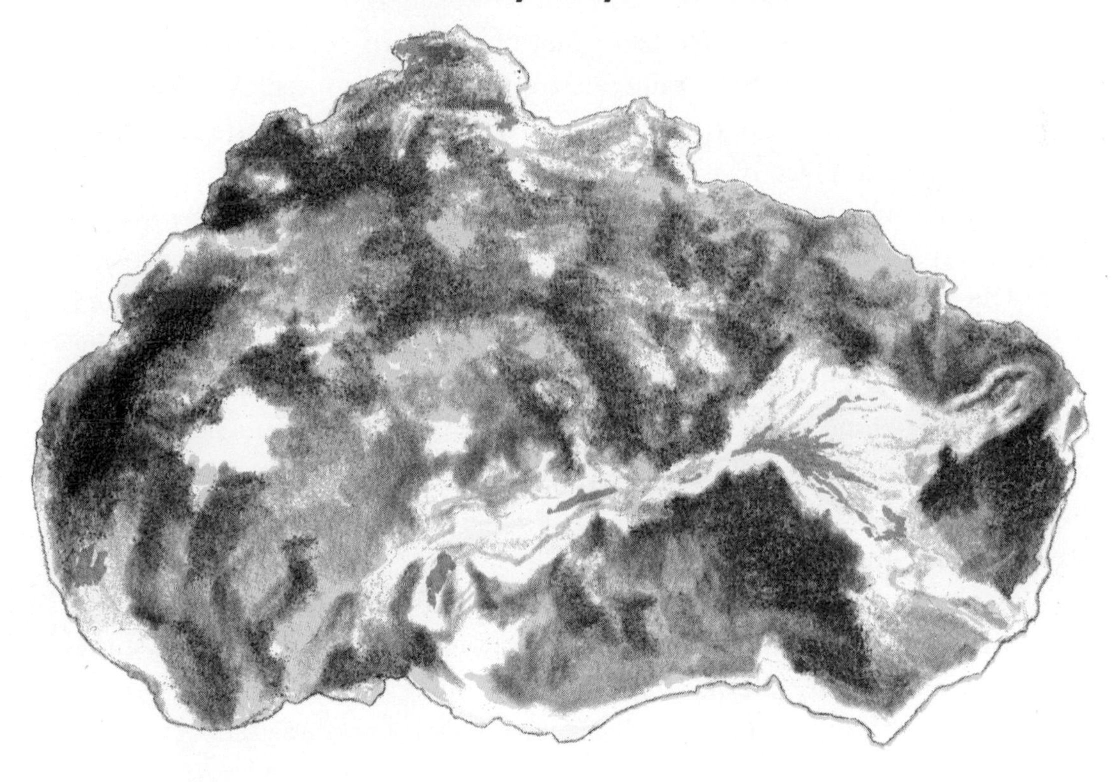

Edited under the supervision of

Dr. Paul E. Blackwood
Washington, D. C.

Text and illustrations approved by

Oakes A. White
Brooklyn Children's Museum
Brooklyn, New York

GROSSET & DUNLAP • Publishers • NEW YORK

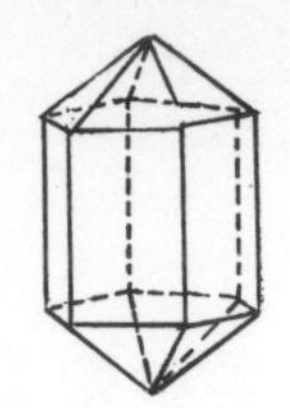 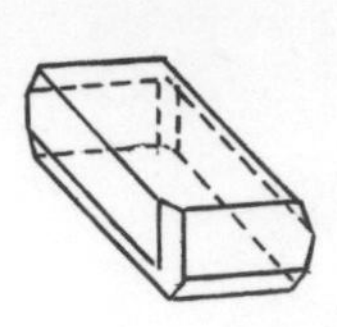 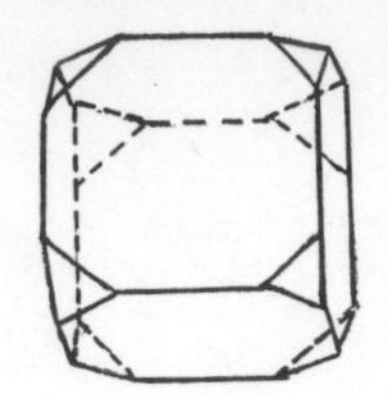 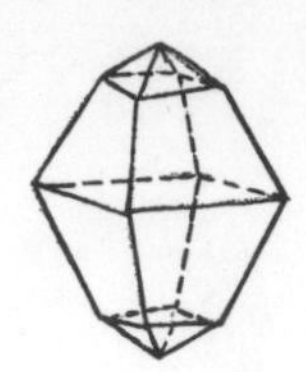 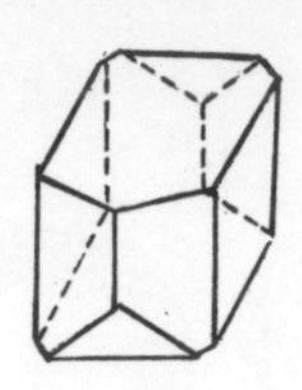

INTRODUCTION

In an age of rockets and missiles, the study of rocks and minerals is no less important — and in this colorful *How and Why Wonder Book,* we see why it is so important. We learn that our modern age of rockets would not even be possible without minerals from the earth's crust. We learn the answers to dozens of important questions about the earth's surface and the changes that take place in it.

Anyone who has ever picked up a rounded pebble, a curiously shaped rock or a sparkling gem and handled it with wonder knows the urge to collect. The chances are that almost everyone who has walked in a field, along a stream or in a park has pocketed a sample of rock or mineral to examine and enjoy later. What is it? How was it made? Is it valuable? This *How and Why Wonder Book* about rocks and minerals is useful because it helps to answer these and other questions. In addition, it tells how to start and how to organize a rock collection. It is a helpful guide for parents and children who want to study rocks together.

Scientists who study the earth's surface are called geologists, and this book will help children explore the big questions which geologists are studying. It surely should take its place with the other *How and Why Wonder Books* on the library shelves of all science-minded young readers.

Paul E. Blackwood

Dr. Blackwood is a professional employee in the U. S. Office of Education. This book was edited by him in his private capacity and no official support or endorsement by the Office of Education is intended or should be inferred.

Library of Congress Catalog Card Number: 61-1514

1971 Printing

Published simultaneously in Canada. Printed in the United States of America.

CONTENTS

THE WORLD OF ROCKS AND MINERALS

What is our earth made of?

ALMOST all of the earth — the hills, the mountains, the ground itself — is made of rocks and minerals.

There are many different kinds, and it would take a long time just to write down all their names. Yet, most of the rocks and minerals on earth are very common.

Sand is a common mineral. It is common because it is found everywhere.

Water is another common mineral. We find it in the streams and in the rivers. It fills the lakes and the seas. Most of the earth is covered with water. The great oceans of the world, together with the streams, rivers and lakes, cover about three-fourths of the surface of the world.

Mixed up in these waters are other minerals. We cannot see them by looking into the water, but they are there just the same. These minerals have been dissolved in the water.

Water is very important because we cannot live without it. It helps to make up an important part of our earth.

LEARNING ABOUT OUR WORLD

Why do we study about rocks and minerals?

WE LIVE in a wonderful world. It is full of interesting things and it is fun to learn about things.

Almost all of our world — even the inside of the world — is made of rocks and minerals. We study them to learn about our world.

Every day we use something made of rocks or minerals. But often they have been changed. They do not look the same.

Glass does not look like sand. Yet glass is made from sand. The ink that printed the letters on this page was made from minerals. We study about rocks and minerals to learn about the things we use every day.

Many people earn their living by working with rocks and minerals, making them into many different things we use. Some people have fun just looking for and finding rocks. It is important to learn about rocks and minerals so we can learn to live better.

We study about rocks and minerals to learn about our world, to learn about the things we use, and to learn to earn a livelihood.

ROCKS

What is a rock?

ROCKS are made of minerals. A few are made of just one mineral, but most of them are made of many minerals. There are many kinds of rocks.

Very small rocks are called sand. Very small sand is like sugar or salt. The individual grains are so small that they are hard to see.

Rocks bigger than sand have other names, like pebbles, or stones. Big rocks are called boulders. Some of them may be as big as a house.

Rocks are big and little. They have different shapes and sizes. Rocks are sometimes round like a ball, or square like a block.

Rocks are of many colors. You can find red rocks, blue rocks and yellow rocks. Often rocks are made of mixed colors. When you look, you can find them of almost every color.

THE SEASHORE, AT LOW TIDE, SHOWING SAND, ROCKS OF DIFFERENT SIZES, AND ROCK CLIFFS IN THE BACKGROUND

A STREAM SHOWING ROCKS WHICH HAVE BEEN SMOOTHED AND ROUNDED BY WATER FLOW

Are rocks found everywhere?

ROCKS are found almost everywhere. The most common place is outdoors on the ground. Most of the ground is made up of big and little rocks.

Rocks are found at the seashore. Even the tiny pieces of sand are countless little rocks that make up the beach. The waves of the ocean wash and roll the sand around.

Outdoors you can find many rocks. You can find rocks in the hills, in the valleys and in rivers and streams.

The rocks in the rivers and streams are smooth and round. The water moves along and pushes them around. The rocks then become smooth and round by rubbing and bumping against each other.

In this way sharp rocks are broken into smaller rocks and in time are made smooth and round. Rocks are being changed all the time by moving water.

MINERALS ARE ALL AROUND US — AT HOME, IN SCHOOL AND OUTDOORS. THE KITCHEN IN YOUR HOME USUALLY HAS MANY THINGS MADE OF MINERALS.

MINERALS

What is a mineral?

A MINERAL is a chemical element or a combination of chemical elements. Minerals are all around us and they are easily found almost everywhere. In fact, it may be said that anything that is not an animal or a vegetable is a mineral.

You should be able to look around as you read this book and see some of these minerals. Can you see a window? The glass is a mineral. Can you see a dish? Can you see any kitchen pots and pans? These and other household articles are made out of minerals, too.

A good part of your wooden pencil is made of minerals. The part that makes the black mark is made of graphite — a mineral. The metal part that holds the eraser is made up of minerals, too, as is the paint on the pencil.

Almost all minerals are solids, but water is a liquid mineral. It is made up of two chemical elements — oxygen and hydrogen.

Some other minerals are clay, chalk and oil. Metals, such as iron, silver and gold are minerals, too. Scientists have found about 2,000 different specimens.

Where can you find minerals?

SOME minerals are found on top of the ground. Others are dug up from under the ground.

Many people go around looking for minerals. Prospectors are men who look for valuable minerals. In many places they have found large deposits. Then a mine may be started, if enough is found in one place. The mineral is then taken out of the mine and sold.

A mine where iron is found is called an iron mine and the mineral taken out is named iron ore. The word "ore" usually refers to any natural material which contains a valuable metal. A gold mine has gold ore and a lead mine has lead ore.

In many cases, more than one kind of ore is found together. Often, for example, silver and lead ores are close together.

All minerals do not come from mines. Some of our important minerals come from the sea. Salt is an important mineral. You use salt in your food. Salt is found both in the sea and on the land.

OPEN PIT IRON MINE

VOLCANOES

THE BEGINNING OF A VOLCANO

THE START OF A LITTLE VOLCANO

What is an active volcano?

AN ACTIVE volcano is one that is said to be "erupting." It shoots out steam, ash and hot rocks. Such a volcano is working and it is active.

Millions of years ago there were many active volcanoes. They were working in many places. Some were working here in America.

A volcano begins deep down in the earth, where it is very hot. It is so hot that the rock has turned into magma — a name for very hot rock.

Deep in the earth there is much hot magma, which is sometimes pushed upward by pressure from the heavy rocks all around it. Finally the hot magma reaches the top of the ground. Here it breaks a little crack or hole in the earth. Steam, ashes and hot rocks come out.

Loud noises come from it as the rocks are blown out. The rocks pile up around the hole and the pile begins to form a cone about the crack in the earth. The cone is made up of rock, ashes and material thrown out of the volcano.

This is the beginning of a little volcano. Day after day it works and grows.

A DORMANT VOLCANO

AN OLD VOLCANO FORMED INTO A MOUNTAIN

The rocks and ashes grow into a big hill. More ashes and hot rocks come out of the hole at the top of it. Another name for this hill is a volcano.

Sometimes the volcano pours out lava. Lava is very hot and is made of hot melted rock, which is also called molten rock.

The old volcano has worked for many years. It has built a large mountain and made some smaller hills close by. The volcano has turned the flat land into hills and mountains.

Other volcanoes have been working, too, helping to build up the land.

Volcanoes that worked many millions of years ago are no longer active. Only the hills and mountains they built long ago remain to tell us that they once existed.

When a volcano has not erupted for a long time, it is dormant. This kind of volcano is known to be inactive. If it is inactive for a very long time, it may be considered dead. Then the volcano is said to be extinct.

IGNEOUS ROCKS—ONE OF

What is an igneous rock?

IGNEOUS is the name of one of the three big groups of rocks. Igneous rocks were made in a special way.

The word igneous means made from fire or heat. Therefore, all igneous rocks have been formed by heat.

Deep down in the earth it is very hot. The rocks and minerals there are very hot. The heat has helped to change these rocks and minerals into molten rock, called magma.

BASALT CLIFF

When the magma comes up to the surface of the earth, it cools off and becomes hard. The cold magma, hardened into rock, is called igneous rock. There are many different kinds of igneous rocks, but all of them have come from the magma found deep in the earth.

Sometimes the magma does not get all the way up to the earth's surface. It cools underneath the ground, turning into rock before it gets to the surface. This kind of igneous rock is called granite.

Huge rocks are formed under the ground in this manner. Sometimes the rocks made in this way are several miles long and almost as wide and deep.

GRANITE

THE THREE BIG GROUPS OF ROCKS

Where do igneous rocks come from?

A GOOD place to find igneous rocks is near old volcanoes. These rocks were made when the volcanoes were still active. Today you can still find the rocks they made.

Many different kinds of rocks are found near the old volcanoes. Lava is one. It is a common igneous rock.

Lava in the form of molten rock pours out of a crack in the side of a volcano. It runs steaming down the side of the volcano and over everything in its path.

RIGHT: AN ERUPTING VOLCANO SHOWING MOLTEN ROCK AND LAVA FLOWING DOWN ITS SIDE. BELOW: IGNEOUS DUMP ROCK FROM VOLCANOES.

In time, the molten lava cools and hardens, turning into igneous rock. The name, lava, can mean the molten rock or even the cold hard rock.

Long ago there were many volcanoes in the western states and some in a few of the eastern states. They were active for many years, throwing out ashes, cinders, rocks and dust. Year after year they worked, building the land higher and higher.

If you live in the West, you can still see where the volcanoes once were active. Today they are extinct. Around and about them you will find many kinds of igneous rocks.

Are there many kinds of igneous rocks?

GRANITE is one of our most common igneous rocks, made deep under the ground.

Granite is made of quartz, feldspar and mica. These are all minerals. Quartz and feldspar are light-colored. They make granite a light-colored rock. The little bits of mica in granite make the dark spots.

Granite may be colored red, pink, yellow or brown. Often it is a mixture of colors in between.

GRANITE

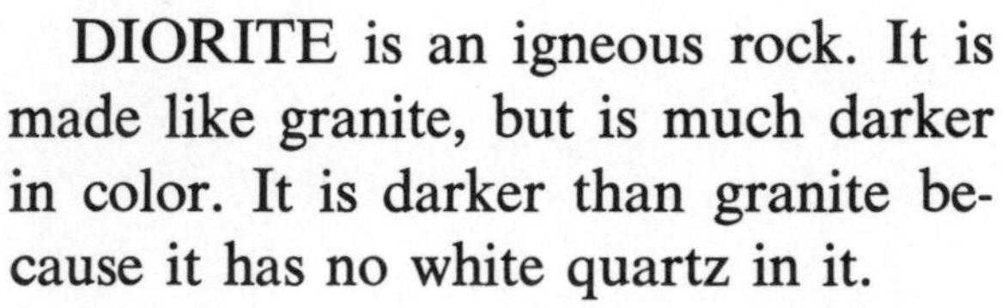

DIORITE is an igneous rock. It is made like granite, but is much darker in color. It is darker than granite because it has no white quartz in it.

Diorite is made of dark minerals — dark feldspars and hornblende.

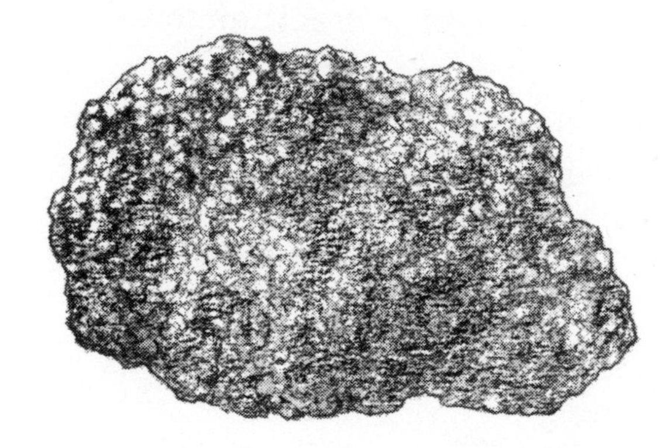

DIORITE

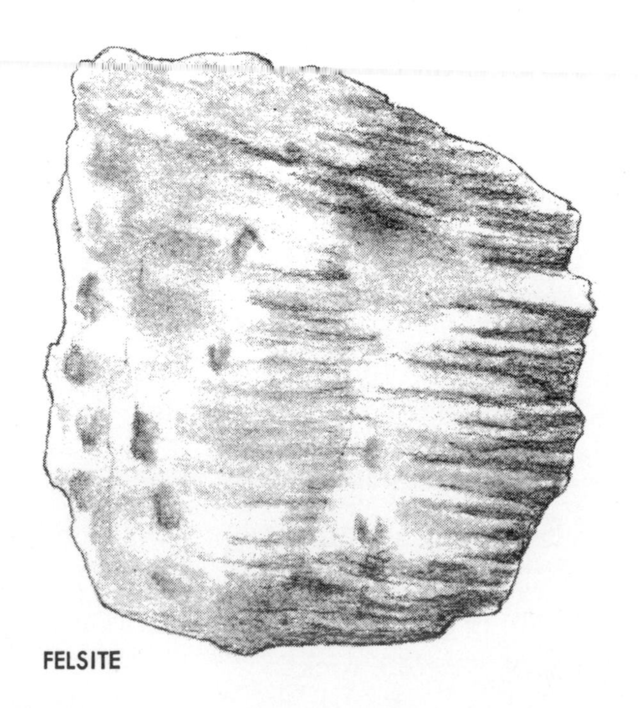

FELSITE

FELSITE rocks are made from fast-cooling lava. The lava cools too fast to turn into granite or basalt. The lava cools too slowly to make obsidian, another kind of igneous rock. It cools just right and turns into felsite.

Felsite rocks are usually made from light-colored lavas. These rocks are often colored light gray, green, yellow or even red.

BASALT is a rock that comes from volcanoes. Sometimes the lava from a volcano is a very dark color. As this dark lava slowly cools, it turns into a black rock called basalt.

Basalt is a very useful igneous rock. It is crushed and sold to make many useful things. Basalt is used in sidewalks, buildings and roads, just like granite.

This kind of rock was formed in giant sheets when the ancient volcanoes poured out huge flows of lava that cooled faster than the granite-forming magmas.

BASALT

OBSIDIAN is another igneous rock made by volcanoes. When lava flows out of the volcano, it often cools very fast and forms a rock called obsidian. This rock looks just like colored glass. It is really natural glass and is found in many colors.

Indians found obsidian very useful. They made the tips of their arrows and spears out of it. The way in which this rock breaks apart makes it easy to shape arrow and spear points.

INDIANS MADE THE TIPS OF THEIR SPEARS AND ARROWS OUT OF OBSIDIAN.

Can you tell how the igneous rocks you have just read about were made?

Granite and diorite were formed when the magma did not reach the surface of the earth. This magma cooled very slowly deep under the earth's surface.

Basalt was made when the magma reached the surface. This magma came out of the earth and we call it lava. The lava cooled into basalt.

Felsite formed from faster cooling lava than basalt. But the fastest cooling lava of all turned into glass. This natural glass we call obsidian.

HEAVY CRANES ARE USED BY WORKERS IN QUARRIES TO LIFT BIG ROCKS. IN THIS GRANITE QUARRY, A MAN GUIDES THE MOVEMENT OF A ROCK WHICH HAS BEEN RAISED UP BY A CRANE.

ROCK QUARRIES

What is a quarry?

A QUARRY is a large open hole in the ground or the side of a hill. It is a place where rocks and stones are dug out.

There are many kinds of rock quarries. One kind will have granite rocks. Another will have sandstone and there are some quarries of marble, too.

Big machines help the workers take the rock out of a granite quarry. The big rocks are used to build many things, but most of the time the builders need more small rocks than big rocks.

Rock-crushing machines take the big rocks and break them into smaller pieces. These small pieces of broken rock are called crushed rock or gravel, which is used to build new roads.

Rock is heavy and expensive to move a long way. Therefore, we find rock quarries close to big cities or new roads where lots of crushed rock is used for construction purposes.

EROSION

Does the earth wear out?

VOLCANOES are land builders. They help to make the land higher. But the land does not stay built up. It keeps wearing away. Day after day and year after year, the wind and the water help to wear away the land.

The wind may blow dirt, sand and soil into a nearby stream. The stream carries the dirt, sand and soil to the sea. Day after day the earth is washed away by running water.

You may have seen a muddy stream or river. It was carrying the earth toward the sea. This is the way the wind and the water are taking away the earth.

Not all streams lead to the sea. Some end in lakes or other streams. These streams carry material into the lakes. In time the lake fills up with mud, dirt, sand and the like. When this happens, the lake turns into a shallow marsh. In time the marsh may dry up. This is another place from which the wind and water may take away the land.

When the land is being moved by the wind or water, we say it is eroding. The process of erosion is going on all of the time. It may be helpful, but more often it is harmful in destroying much valuable land.

ON SEACOASTS, OCEAN WAVES ERODE THE LAND. THE WAVES CARRY LOOSE BITS OF ROCK. THESE BITS OF ROCK, PLUS THE FORCE OF THE WAVES AGAINST THE LAND, WEAR AWAY THE EARTH.

SEDIMENTARY ROCKS

Are there rocks under the water?

STIR up a handful of dirt in a glass of water. At first the water will be cloudy. But if the water is left alone, the dirt will settle to the bottom of the glass. In time the water will be clear again.

The dirt that has settled to the bottom of the glass is called sediment. From this word comes the name sedimentary, the name for the second big group of rocks.

This kind of rock was formed by sediment from rivers and streams. Every day the streams and rivers bring more and more mud, sand and rock to the seas. These settle to the bottom and are called sediment.

The big rocks settle first. They sink first because they are bigger and heavier. Next the sand and then the mud sinks to the bottom of the sea. In this way different layers are built up. The layers build up on the sea bottom year after year until they are very thick.

BODIES OF WATER HOLD MUD, SAND AND ROCKS, AS WELL AS LIVING THINGS, INCLUDING PLANTS AND SEA ANIMALS. MANY OBJECTS SINK IN THE WATER — SOME TO THE VERY BOTTOM, OTHERS ONLY PARTWAY. IN TIME, THERE ARE LAYERS OF ROCK, SAND AND MUD IN THE WATER.

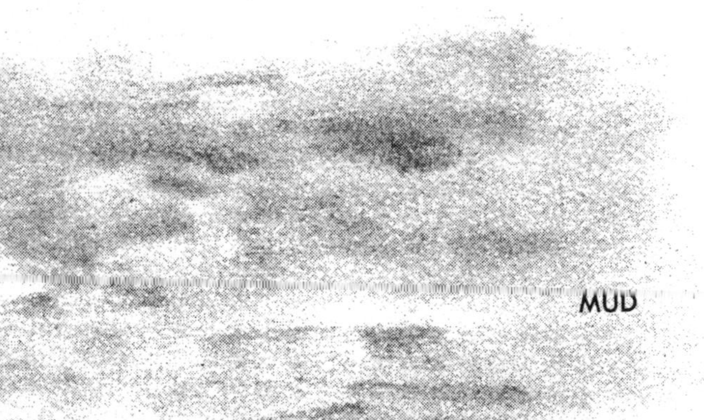

VOLCANIC TUFF IS SEDIMENTARY ROCK. TUFF IS COMPOSED OF MANY LAYERS OF VOLCANIC ASHES AND DUST. THESE LAYERS BUILT UP AROUND ACTIVE VOLCANOES.

The weight of the layers of sand and water above press down on the bottom layer of sand. This bottom layer begins to change.

Each tiny grain of sand begins to stick to another one. The sand grains change into stone. Because the stone is made from sand, we call it sandstone. Sandstone is a sedimentary rock.

Most sedimentary rock is made under the water in lakes or seas and in the oceans. But sometimes sedimentary rock is made on dry land!

For instance, long ago, many volcanoes blew out ashes and volcanic dust which settled around them. Year after year the layers built up. In time another kind of rock was made — sedimentary rock called volcanic tuff.

In the West, large areas are covered with this kind of rock. The different layers are of different colors, making a colorful sedimentary rock.

How are rocks made?

NOT ALL sedimentary rocks were made from dirt and sand that came down the river. Some were made from the shells of sea animals and plants.

Millions of animals live in the sea. Some of them build a hard shell which is made of lime, and this protects the animal living inside. Clams and snails live in shells.

Some plants have shells, too. A diatom is a tiny plant that lives in a shell. Millions and millions of tiny shelled diatoms live in the sea.

When a plant or animal dies, its shell sinks to the bottom of the sea. After many years, millions of dead shells pile up on the bottom of the sea. Again, the top layer pushes down on the bottom layers. The shells in the bottom layer are pushed close together.

The weight of the shells on top changes the bottom layer of shells. The shell layer at the bottom turns into stone. The name of this stone is limestone, which is another kind of sedimentary rock.

Look again at the word limestone. Do you see that the first part of the word says lime? This tells us what the rock is made of. The last part of the word tells us the lime has turned into stone.

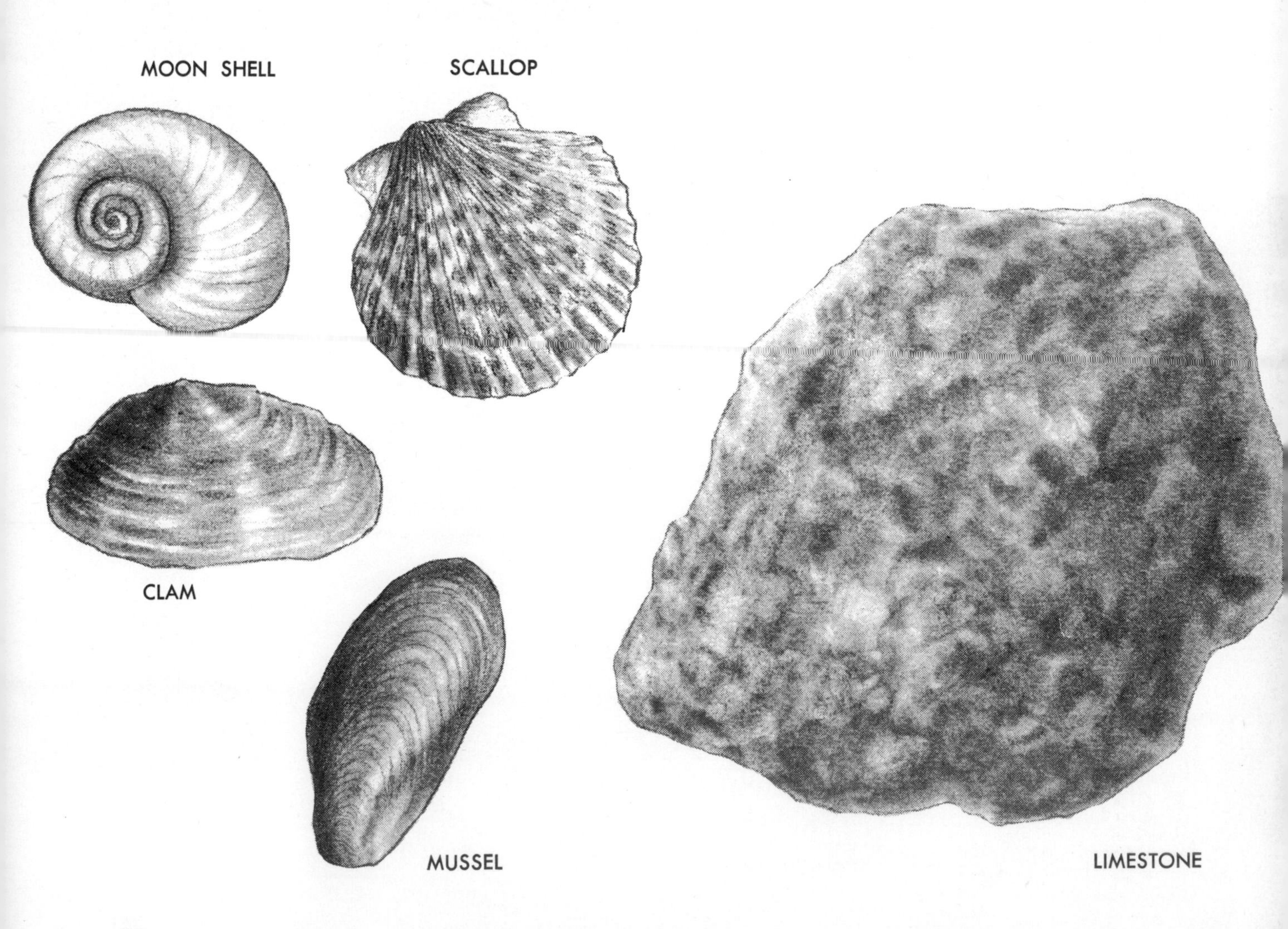

Where are sedimentary rocks found?

SEDIMENTARY rocks were formed under the seas and oceans. The sedimentary rocks built up higher and higher in some places. This made the sea bottom rise higher and higher.

Millions of years went by. In some places the sea bottom rose slowly. If it rose high enough, it came out of the water.

The land that came out of the water was made of sediment. Below the top layers of sediment were sedimentary rocks. You can see these rocks today near the seashore.

NEAR THE SEASHORE, YOU CAN SEE SEDIMENTARY ROCK. LAYERS OF SEDIMENT DEPOSITS IN THE WATER ROSE HIGHER AND HIGHER. AFTER MANY YEARS, SEDIMENTARY ROCK EMERGED FROM THE WATER.

SEDIMENTARY ROCK THAT CAME OUT OF THE WATER OFTEN ROSE TO GREAT HEIGHT. YOU CAN SEE HOW LAYERS OF SEDIMENT WERE BUILT UP AS YOU DRIVE ALONG HIGHWAYS WHICH CUT THROUGH HILLS MADE OF SEDIMENTARY ROCK.

Wherever you find land that was once under water, you are almost sure to find sedimentary rock.

Roads are often cut through hills. If the hill is made of sedimentary rock, it will show the layers. You can usually find sedimentary rocks in hills that are layered.

Sedimentary rocks are very common and may be found almost everywhere. The midwestern part of our country is covered with sedimentary rocks. Large areas of the East are made of this type of rock. The West also has its share of sedimentary deposited rock.

Are there many kinds of sedimentary rocks?

CONGLOMERATE is a sedimentary rock. It is made of a mixture of smooth round stones and pebbles. The larger stones in a conglomerate rock are held together by another kind of stone, either limestone or sandstone.

Conglomerate rock is made in old streams and river beds. The large stones are washed down the stream. Then, in a quiet pool, the rocks sink to the bottom and pile up.

More rocks and sand continue to pile up in the old stream bed. In time the big and little rocks become changed into conglomerate rock.

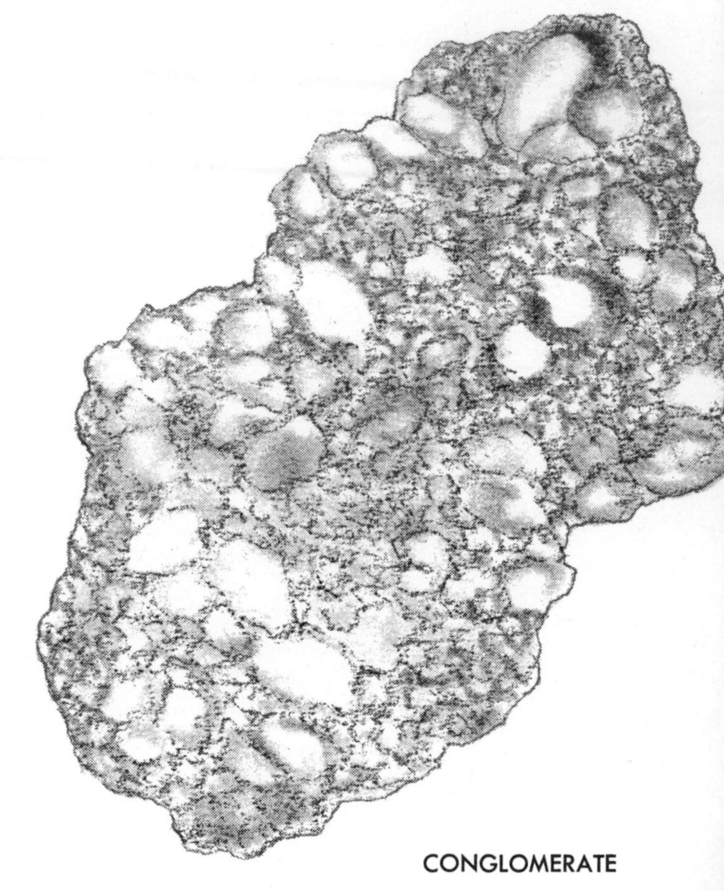

CONGLOMERATE

SANDSTONE

SANDSTONE is a very useful sedimentary rock. It is used in walls and buildings, because it is strong and easy to quarry. After it has been taken from the quarry, it is cut into blocks and used in the building of things.

There are many different colors of sandstone. Brown is common. In some places so much sandstone is colored brown it is called brownstone. You can also find yellow-colored, gray-colored and red-colored sandstones.

SHALE

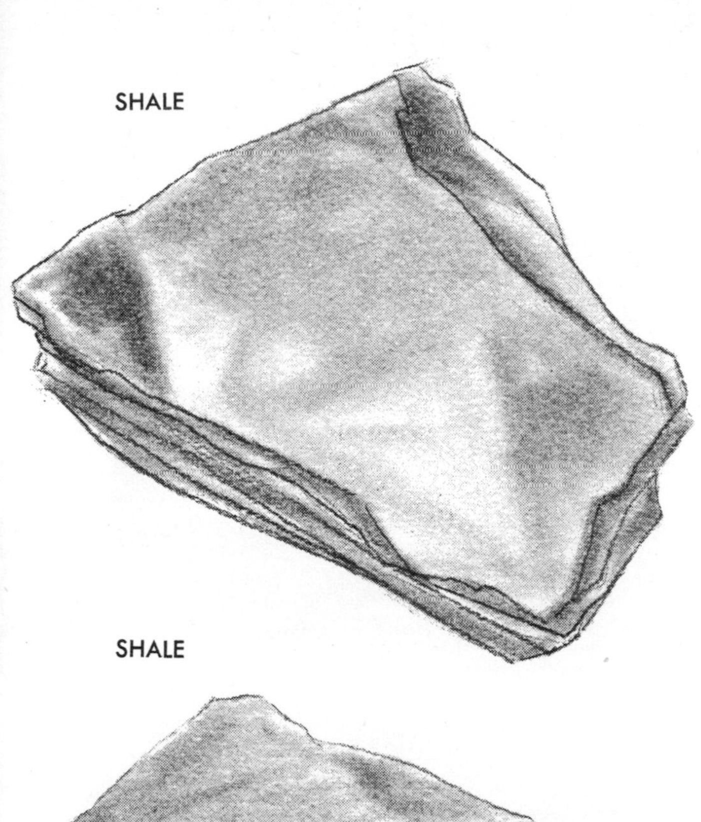

SHALE

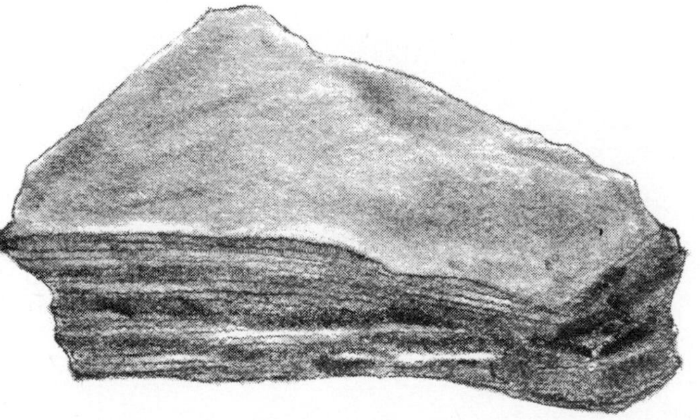

SHALE is made from fine silt and mud. Another name for it is mudstone. Yet, sometimes it is so soft, it is not like a stone at all.

Most rocks do not have any odor, but wet shale does. It smells like damp earth.

You can find shales of many different colors. Red, brown and gray are common colors of shale. The color, of course, depends upon the color of the mud or fine silt from which the shale was made.

LIMESTONE

LIMESTONE is a sedimentary rock that forms only under water. It takes millions of years to make a lot of limestone. Some deposits of limestone are thousands of feet thick!

Pure limestone is clean and white. But often other things get mixed into the limestone that may change its color. When a little bit of iron gets mixed into it, the white limestone changes to yellow or brown. Other materials can change the color of limestone to green, gray, black and many other colors.

DOLOMITE

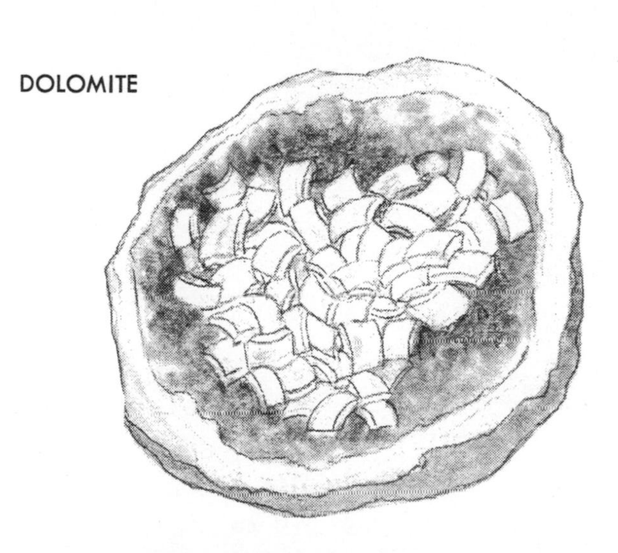

DOLOMITE is another kind of limestone made under the sea. It is usually white or light-colored. One kind of dolomite breaks up easily. This kind looks just like white rice!

METAMORPHIC ROCKS

LIMESTONE

SHALE

MARBLE

SLATE

Why do rocks have different shapes and colors?

THE NAME metamorphic means "to have been changed." This name is used to tell about rocks that have been changed in some way. This is the third and last big group of rocks.

Metamorphic rocks began as one kind of rock and later were changed into another kind. All of them began once as igneous or sedimentary rocks. The new rocks do not look the same, for in becoming metamorphic rocks their structure and often their color change.

Sedimentary rocks are formed deep under the seas. After they have been formed, they may become very hot. Heat helps to change sedimentary rocks.

The weight of the rocks and water on top of the sedimentary rocks is very great. The heavy weight or pressure also helps to change the sedimentary rocks. Heat and pressure together change the sedimentary rocks into metamorphic rocks.

When limestone is changed, it turns into marble. If shale is changed, it turns into slate. Both marble and slate are metamorphic rocks.

THE HEAT AND HEAVY WEIGHT, OR PRESSURE, ON SEDIMENTARY AND IGNEOUS ROCKS HELP TO CHANGE THEM INTO METAMORPHIC ROCKS. AS A VOLCANO PUSHES ITS WAY UP THROUGH THE EARTH, GREAT HEAT IS CREATED. AS THE VOLCANO PASSES THROUGH A SEDIMENTARY LAYER, THE HEAT CHANGES THE SEDIMENTARY ROCK INTO METAMORPHIC ROCK.

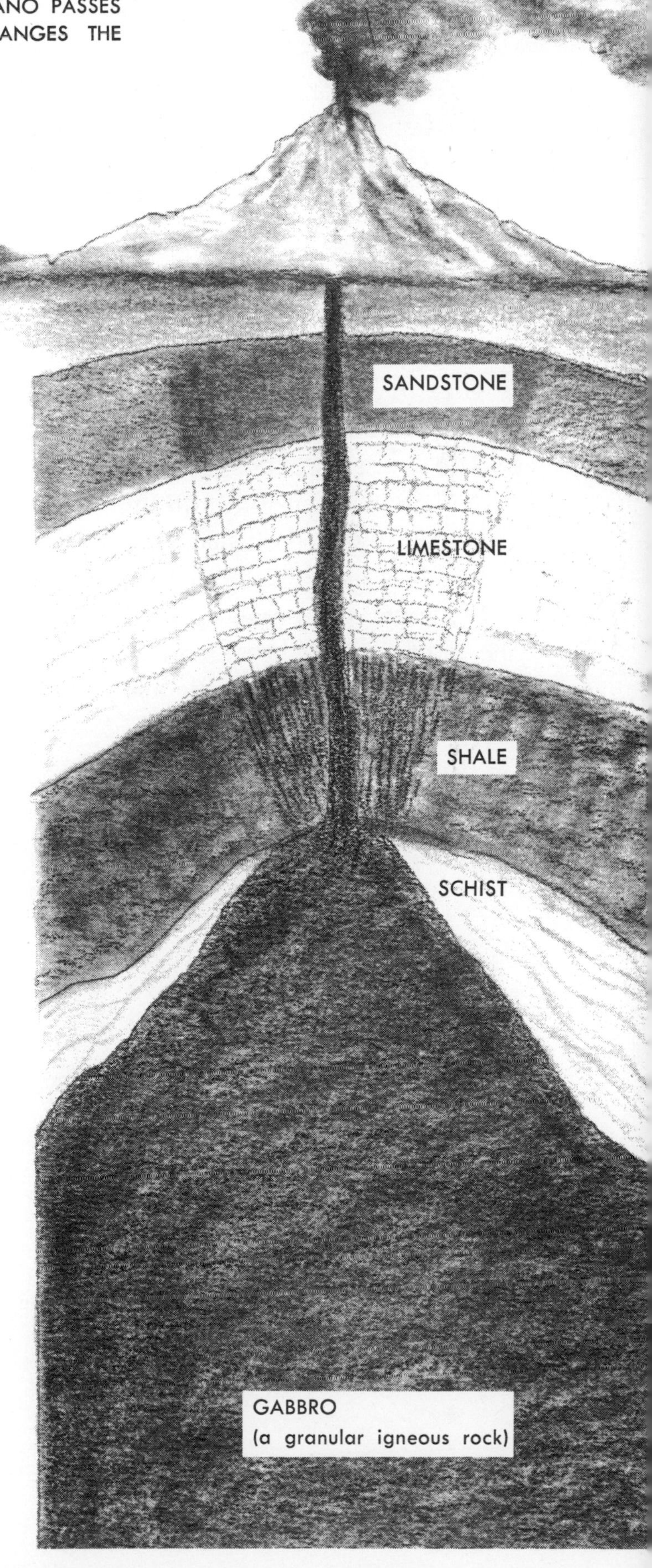

Where do metamorphic rocks come from?

SEDIMENTARY rocks are made deep under the seas and ocean bottoms. Sometimes a sea goes dry. The land moves up and the sedimentary rocks are exposed.

In time the wind and rain wear down the top layers of rock. Then another kind of rock is exposed. The rock exposed is metamorphic rock.

To find metamorphic rock, you must visit a place where the land has been wearing down for many years. There are places in the eastern United States and a few in the West where one can see this kind of rock. There are also many metamorphic rocks far north in Canada.

Sometimes metamorphic rocks can be found where old volcanoes once stood. The red hot lava from them often changed other rocks into metamorphic rocks.

This type of metamorphic rock could occur where the volcano pushed its way up through the earth, passing through a sediment layer on the way. Here the heat helped to change the sedimentary rock into metamorphic rock.

Are there many kinds of metamorphic rocks?

SLATE is a metamorphic rock made from the sedimentary rock shale. When shale is changed by heat and pressure, it turns into slate.

Slate and shale have the same colors, but they do not look alike. They look different because of how they break. The way that they break helps to tell them apart.

Slate breaks into smooth flat sheets of rock. You can split it into very thin pieces, which make fine steppingstones.

The finest blackboards are made of slate that has been split into thin sheets. One side is then polished very smooth before it is used for a blackboard.

Shale will not break into smooth flat sheets of rock. It breaks only into odd shapes. This stone has little use because of the way in which it breaks.

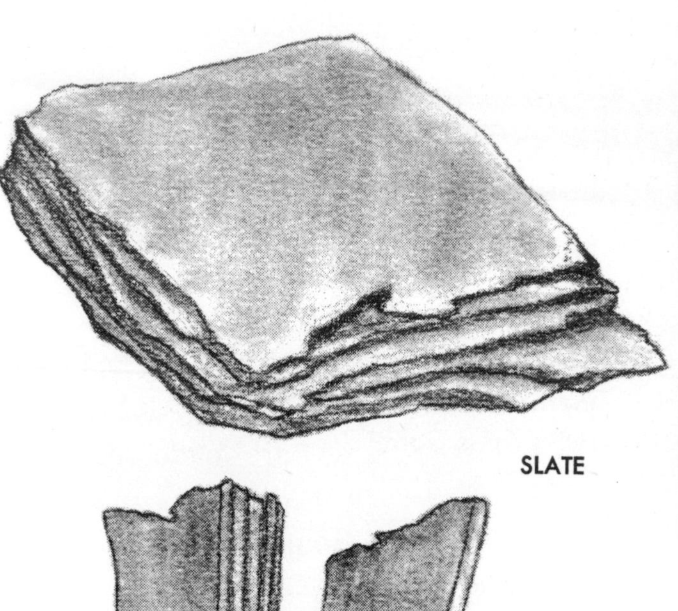

SLATE

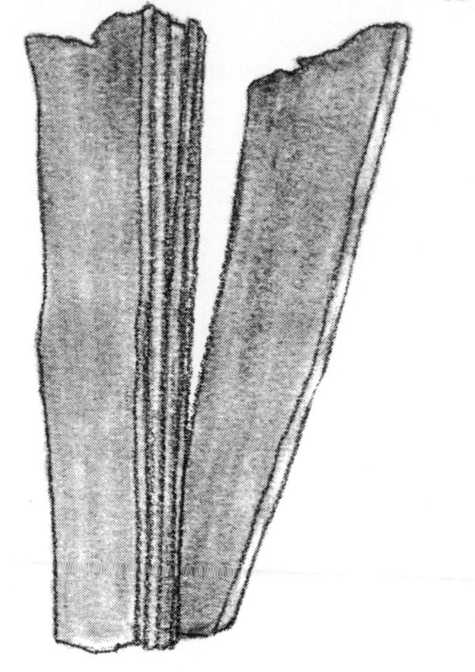

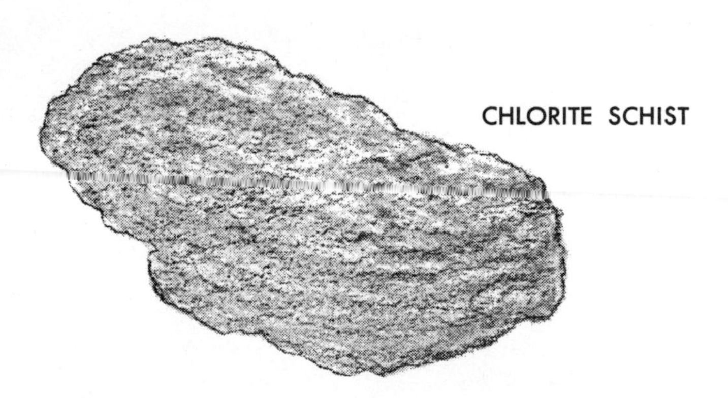

CHLORITE SCHIST

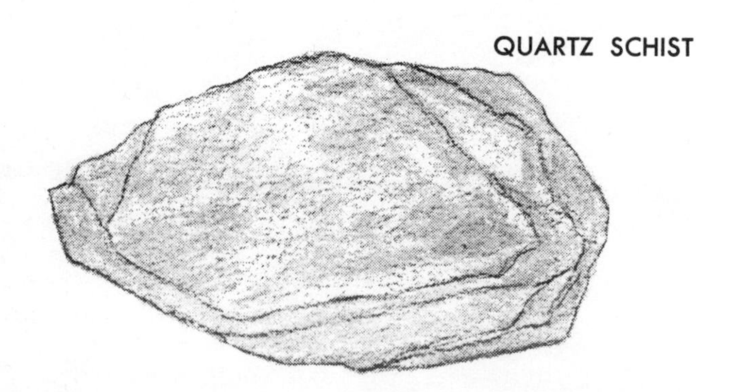

QUARTZ SCHIST

SCHIST is a metamorphic rock made from mudstone or shale. Rock must be changed many times in order to make schist.

As schist is made, some of the minerals in it change. These minerals then become mica and all are turned the same way. The little bits of mica make the schist shine and sparkle.

SERPENTINE

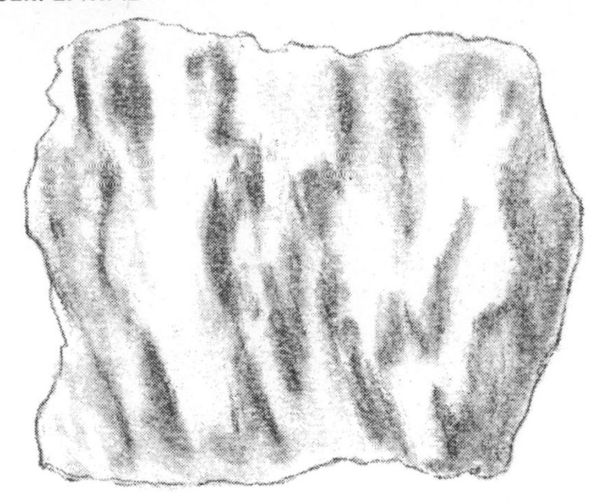

SERPENTINE is a metamorphic rock often colored green. Some serpentine rocks are light green and some are dark green. This stone is slippery to touch. It feels as if it were covered with wax or soap.

When this rock is exposed to the weather, it soon breaks down and crumbles away.

QUARTZITE

QUARTZITE is a very hard metamorphic rock made from hard sandstone.

Pressure and heat changed the sandstone into hard quartzite. Some quartzite is colored like sandstone. These colors are yellow, brown, pink and red.

BLACK MARBLE

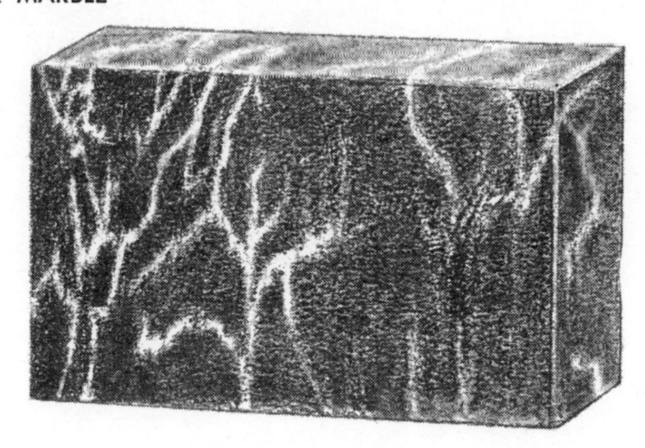

WHITE MARBLE

MARBLE is a metamorphic rock. It comes from limestone that has been changed by heat and pressure. Marble is made-over limestone.

Marble is often many different colors. You can find white marble or black marble or just about any color in between. Often the marble is striped or marked with several colors. Minerals, or impurities, in the marble change its color.

This stone is used in some of the great public buildings in our country. Many beautiful monuments are made with this useful stone.

AMAZONITE (or Amazon stone)

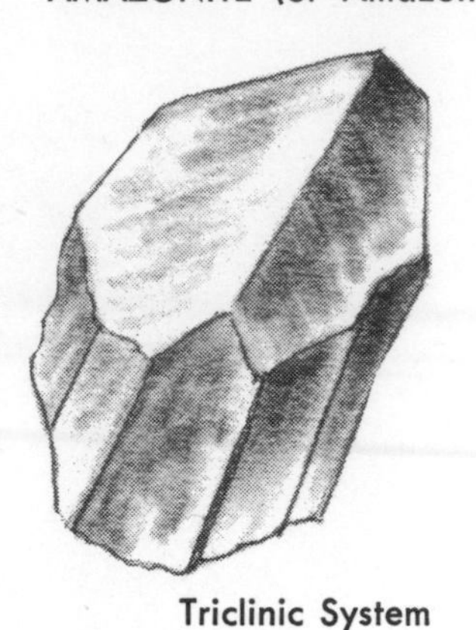

Triclinic System

EPIDOTE

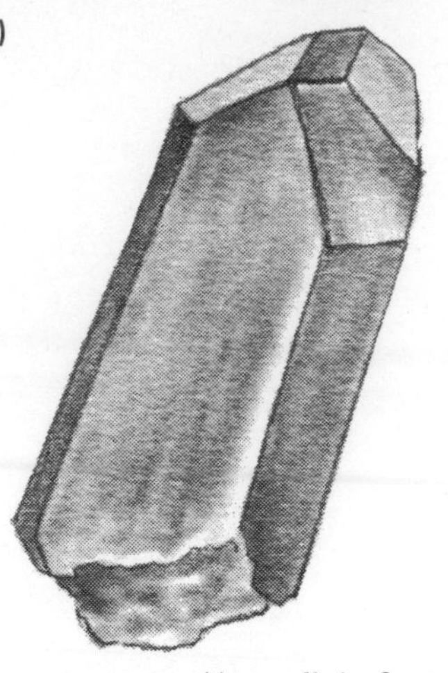

Monoclinic System

SULPHUR

Orthorhombic System

CRYSTALS

What is a crystal?

THERE are non-living substances which grow into bodies of various shapes. They grow by adding on more layers of the same substance, keeping the same shape at all times. These bodies of various shapes are called crystals. Most solid substances, like minerals, are crystalline; that is, they are made up of crystals. So a crystal is really another form of rocks and minerals, except that the word "crystal" tells us that the rock or mineral is of a certain shape.

These different crystal shapes, which help us to tell the minerals apart, are grouped into six main kinds or systems: Cubic System, Tetragonal System, Hexagonal System, Orthorhombic System, Monoclinic System and Triclinic System. Examples of the six different shapes may be seen in the crystal forms shown on this page.

When minerals are first formed, they often turn into crystals. It takes a long time to make big crystals, but some little crystals can be made in two days.

CALCITE

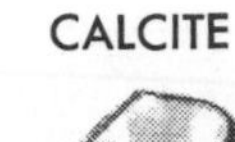

Hexagonal System

RUTILE

Tetragonal System

HALITE (salt)

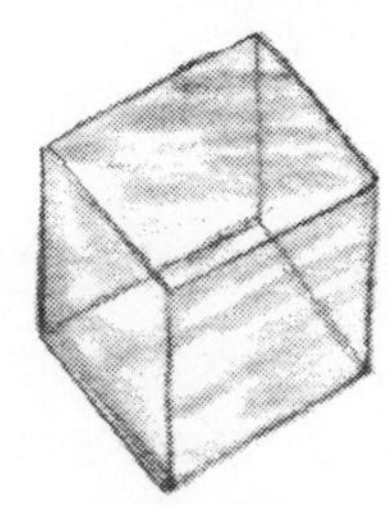

Cubic System

How can you make a crystal?

HERE is a way to make some crystals of your own. Salt crystals are easy to make.

Stir three tablespoons full of salt into a cup of warm water. As you stir the water, the salt will disappear. In a few minutes you will not be able to see the salt crystals. They have disappeared into the water.

Next pour the salty water into a pie pan. Set the pan where it will be warm. Salt crystals will grow faster in a warm place.

Now you must wait for the water to evaporate. This may take a few days. Little by little the water will disappear.

Every day look at the pan of salt water. Soon white crystals will begin to form around the edge of the pan. The white crystals are made of salt.

Sugar crystals can be made in the same way. Even bigger crystals than sugar or salt can be made by dissolving alum crystals. When they turn back into crystals again, you will be surprised at their size. You can buy alum at any drugstore for a few cents.

MINERAL FOODS

Where does the salt we eat come from?

MUCH OF our salt is made near the seashore, in large flat ponds filled with sea water. This water contains lots of salt.

Day after day the hot sun shines and warms the sea water in the pond. Warm sea water helps the salt crystals to form.

As each day goes by, a little more water disappears by evaporation. Salt crystals form in the water that is left.

After many days, the sea water is all gone and only the salt is left behind. The salt has formed as white crystals on the bottom of the dry pond.

When the pond is dry, workmen can gather the salt. The salt is put into little boxes for us to use. Everyone uses salt crystals left behind by the sea water.

Many years ago salt was difficult to get in some countries. Workmen have even been paid wages with salt, instead of money!

This kind of salt has another name — halite. Halite is the mineral name for salt, but most of the time halite is just called salt.

SALT PONDS USED IN THE EVAPORATION OF SEA WATER

Can we eat minerals?

YOU MAY be surprised to learn that every day you eat many different minerals besides salt. These minerals are very helpful to you.

Water is a very common mineral. It is the most important mineral you use. Some of it is in the food you eat. Other water is in the milk you drink. Your body needs some water every day.

You only need to eat very tiny amounts of the other minerals which are found in foods. They cannot be seen because there are only tiny bits of them. But they are very important.

Iron is an important mineral used to make cars and other things. It is also a mineral you need to eat. It is found in eggs and liver. Calcium is a mineral found in cheese, and it helps to make strong bones. Iodine is a mineral needed to keep your body healthy. Iodine is often mixed with the salt you eat.

All of these minerals and many more are found in the food you eat. You need to eat many different kinds of food because each kind has different minerals. They help you to build a healthy body.

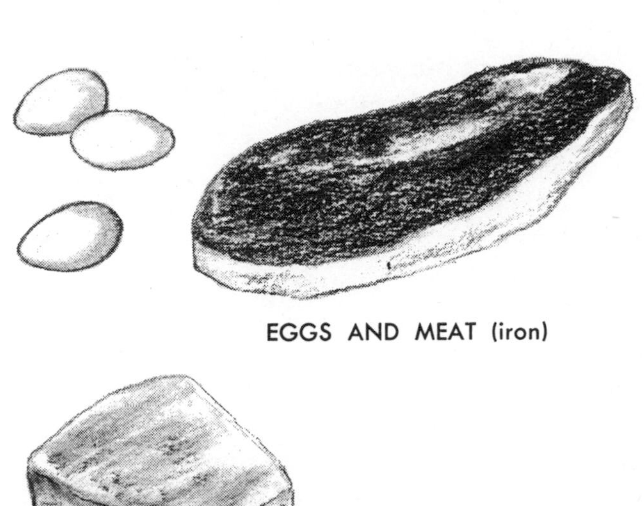

EGGS AND MEAT (iron)

CHEESE (calcium)

SALT (iodine)

FISH (phosphorus)

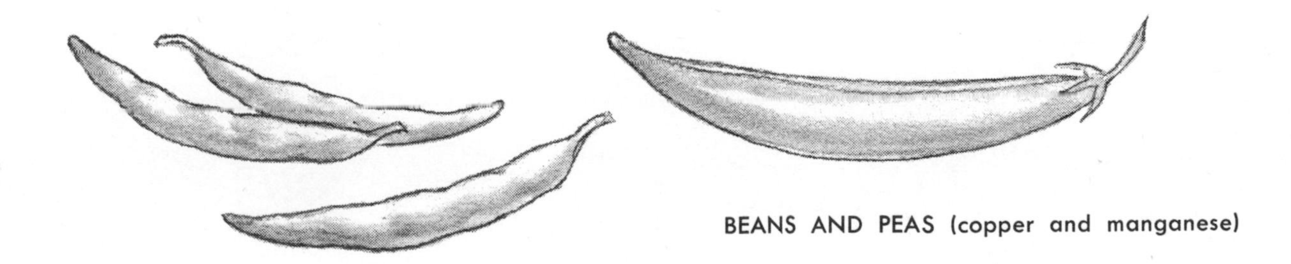

BEANS AND PEAS (copper and manganese)

ROCK-FORMING MINERALS

What are some of the rock-forming minerals?

ROCKS are made from one or more kinds of minerals. Granite is a rock made from three kinds of minerals — quartz, feldspar and mica.

Quartz, feldspar and mica are rock-forming minerals. They are called that because they make rocks, like granite.

QUARTZ is one of the most common rock-forming minerals and is found in all the big groups of rocks — igneous, sedimentary and metamorphic rocks.

Some quartz is colorless, like ice. Other colors are white, pink, violet and gray. Sometimes the dark-colored quartz is called smoky quartz. It looks like the color of dark smoke.

You can find quartz very easily. The small sand grains in dirt are often quartz. Beach sand is usually full of quartz grains. It is found in most igneous rocks, often in the form of crystals.

In fact, the names of many minerals and rocks depend upon whether or not quartz is present in the sample. You should consider quartz to be one of the most important rock-forming minerals.

ROCK CRYSTAL IN DRUSY QUARTZ

CITRINE QUARTZ

SMOKY QUARTZ

ROSE QUARTZ

AMETHYST QUARTZ

FELDSPAR is a very common rock-forming mineral, like quartz. But the name feldspar is really a family name. That is, it is a name used for six or seven different feldspar minerals.

All of these feldspar minerals are much alike, sometimes so much so that it is hard to tell them apart. It is easier to just call them feldspar. So feldspar is the family name given to all of them.

Feldspar minerals occur in almost all of the igneous rocks. Often the color of the rock depends upon the color of the feldspar mixed into it.

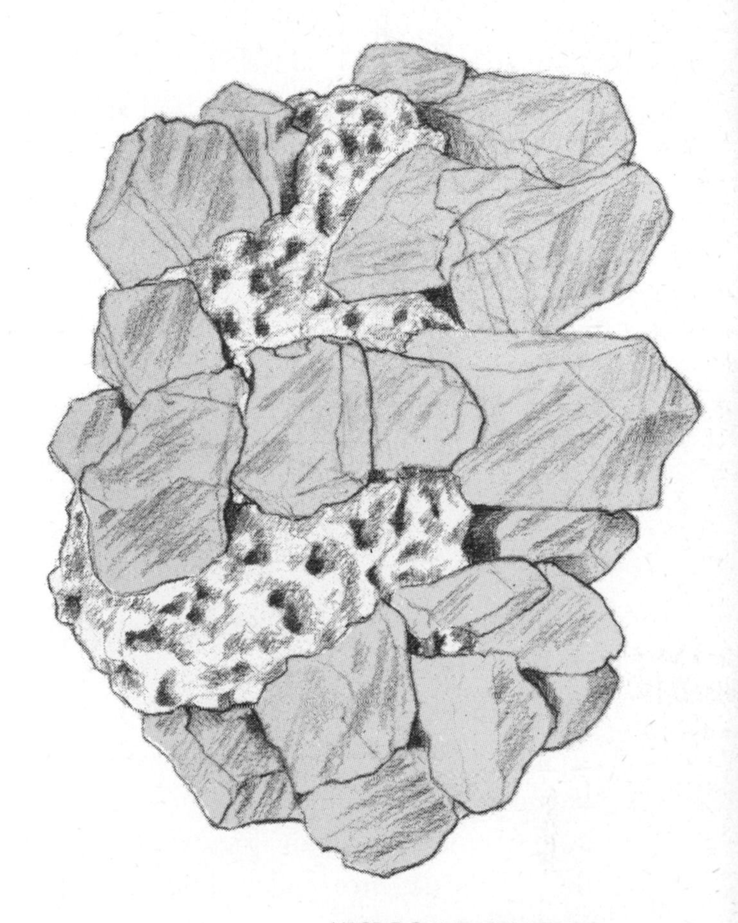

MICROCLINE FELDSPAR

GRANITE WITH PINK FELDSPAR

GRANITE WITH WHITE FELDSPAR

Feldspar may be colored white, light pink or even green. The white and pink colors are the ones you will see most often.

Granite with pink feldspar will look pink. If the feldspar is white, the granite will look white. The quartz in the granite helps to change the color, too.

As granite grows old and is exposed to the weather, it begins to fall apart. We say that it is beginning to decompose. Actually, it is the feldspar in the granite that is breaking apart. In time the wind and water help to change the feldspar into clay.

IDENTIFICATION OF ROCKS AND MINERALS

How do we begin to identify rocks and minerals?

THERE ARE several ways to identify rocks and minerals. First you will have to make some tests. These tests are easy to do and will help you to know more about rocks and minerals.

Each test you make will tell you more about your new rock, until at last you will be able to tell the rock's name.

You must not expect to be able to name every new rock or mineral at first. In the beginning you will be able to name only a few. It takes a long time to learn most of the names of the rocks and minerals.

One of the first tests you will make is to ask yourself, "Where did this rock come from?" Is it an igneous rock? Or does it look more like a sedimentary rock? It might be even a metamorphic rock!

You would first like to know what general kind of rock it is. When you know where it came from, you can often tell what general kind it is.

Once you know if it is an igneous, sedimentary or metamorphic rock, you can make some other tests.

GRANITE IS AN IGNEOUS ROCK COLORED RED, PINK, YELLOW OR BROWN. IT IS USED OFTEN IN CONSTRUCTION WORK.

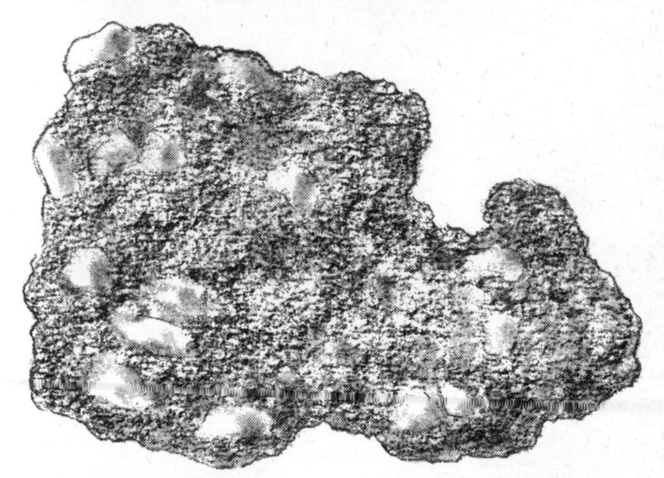

CONGLOMERATE IS A SEDIMENTARY ROCK MADE OF STONES AND PEBBLES, HELD TOGETHER BY LIMESTONE OR SANDSTONE. LIMESTONE IS OFTEN WHITE AND SANDSTONE IS USUALLY BROWN.

MARBLE IS A METAMORPHIC ROCK USUALLY STRIPED OR MARKED WITH SEVERAL COLORS. IT COMES FROM LIMESTONE. MARBLE IS WIDELY USED IN MONUMENTS.

IN THE FIELD, THERE ARE SOME SIMPLE WAYS TO TEST THE HARDNESS OF ROCKS AND MINERALS.

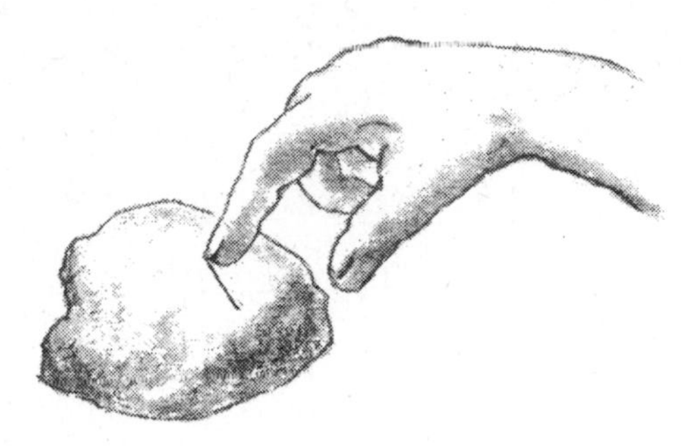

YOUR FINGERNAIL CAN SCRATCH TWO MINERALS — TALC AND GYPSUM.

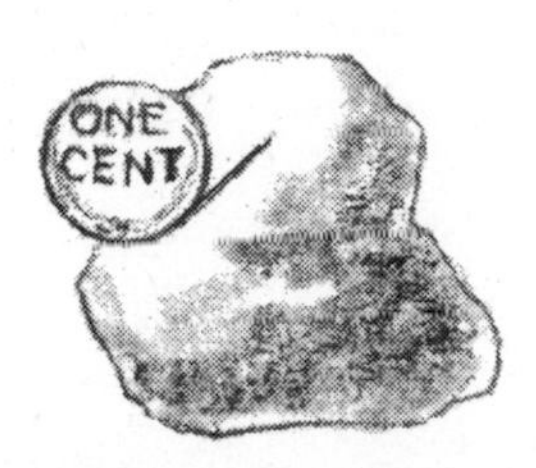

A PENNY IS HARDER THAN YOUR FINGERNAIL AND CAN SCRATCH CALCITE, AS WELL AS TALC AND GYPSUM.

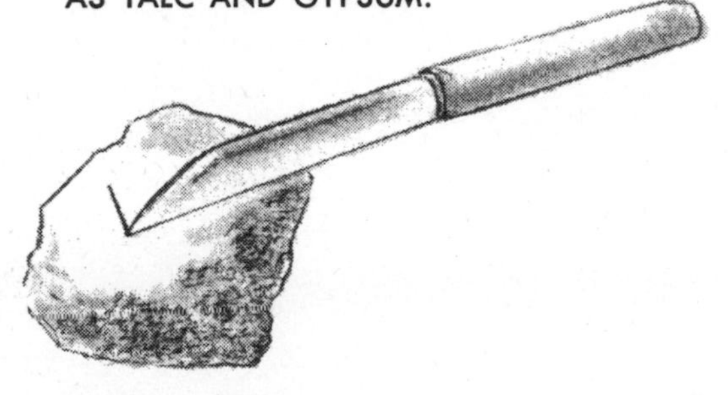

THE BLADE OF A SMALL POCKET KNIFE IS HARDER THAN A PENNY. IT CAN SCRATCH FLUORITE AND APATITE, AS WELL AS THE MINERALS BELOW THEM ON THE SCALE.

HARDER MINERALS CAN SCRATCH THE SOFTER ONES, AND EACH MINERAL CAN SCRATCH ANOTHER OF ITS KIND.

How can you tell how hard a rock or mineral is?

ONE of the most important tests you can make on a specimen is to find out how hard it is. Hardness tells you how easy it is to scratch one mineral with another. Some minerals are very soft. Others are very hard.

If you know how hard or soft a specimen is, it will help you to tell it apart from other minerals.

Geologists, for a long time, have used ten minerals to test for hardness. These ten minerals are called the *Scale of Hardness* minerals.

Each mineral on the scale has a number as well as a name. You have already read about the names of some, and others will be new to you.

There are also some common things that will help you to test for hardness. One of these testers you have with you all of the time — your fingernail — which will scratch at least two minerals. A penny can also be used to scratch certain minerals, and a small pocket knife is another common tester. Its blade will scratch still other minerals. Each mineral can also scratch itself. You will read about these and others in the discussion about the *"Scale of Hardness"* minerals, beginning on the next page.

These minerals have been arranged in order. The softest mineral is number one and the hardest is number ten. Those minerals in between will vary, each higher-numbered mineral being harder than the one before.

THE SCALE OF HARDNESS MINERALS

What are the hardness minerals?

N*UMBER 1. TALC:* Talc is a metamorphic mineral. It is the softest of the minerals in the scale. You can scratch talc with your fingernail.

Talcum powder is made from ground-up talc. Of course, the nice smell is put in after the talc is ground up.

FOLIATED TALC ON SERPENTINE

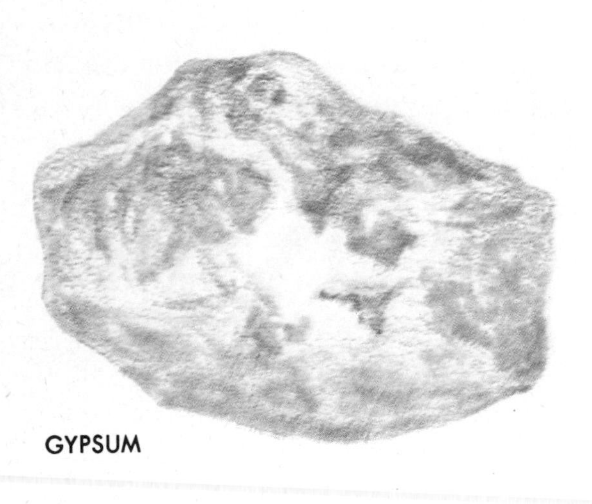
GYPSUM

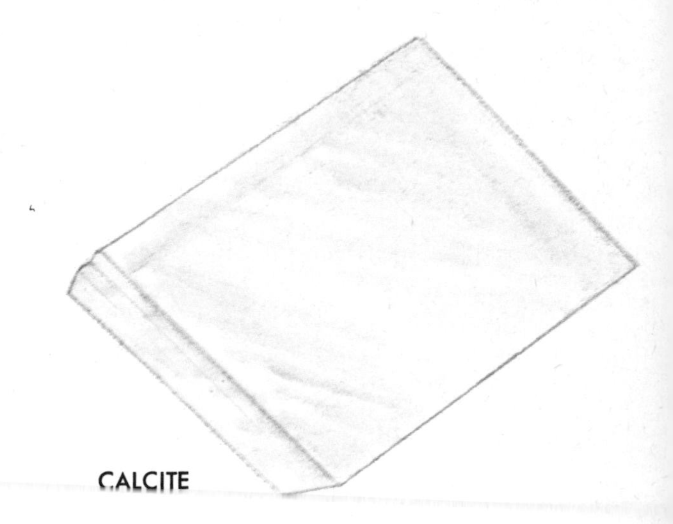
CALCITE

Number 2. GYPSUM: Gypsum is a sedimentary mineral. It is harder than talc, but you can still scratch it with your fingernail.

Gypsum may be colorless or white. It is found in huge beds in the ground where it is dug out. Gypsum is an important mineral. Plaster of Paris is made from it. Plaster wallboard is also made from gypsum. Did you know that the blackboard chalk you use in school was made from gypsum?

Number 3. CALCITE: Calcite is third in the hardness scale. It scratches talc and gypsum. You can scratch calcite with a penny.

Calcite is a colorless or white mineral. You will find it in many places and with all groups of rocks.

A special form of calcite is Iceland Spar. When you look through a clear crystal of Iceland Spar, everything suddenly looks double!

FLUORITE

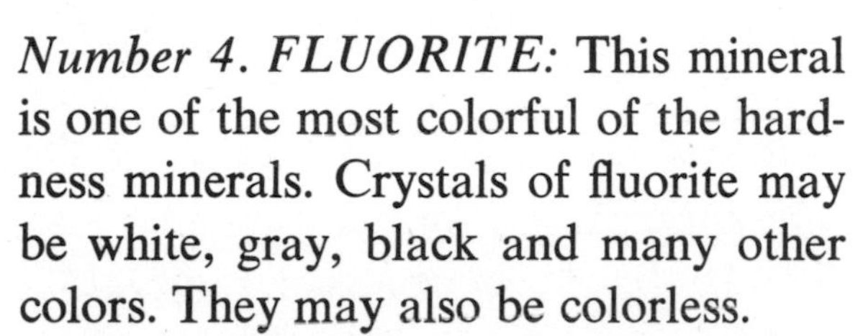

Number 4. FLUORITE: This mineral is one of the most colorful of the hardness minerals. Crystals of fluorite may be white, gray, black and many other colors. They may also be colorless.

Fluorite is four on the hardness scale, but you can scratch it with a small pocket knife.

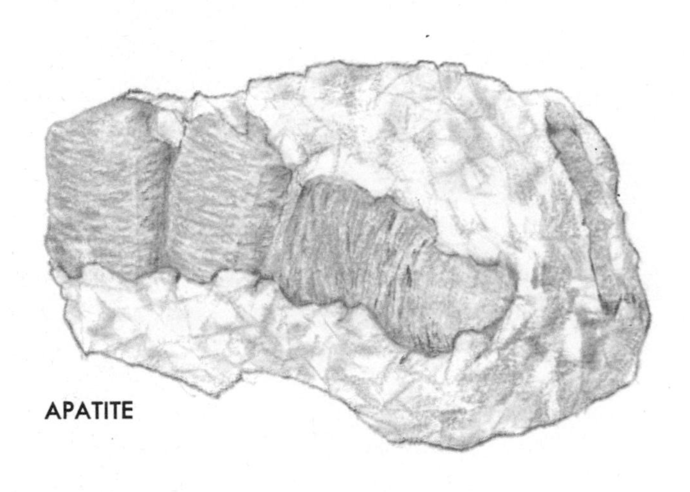

APATITE

Number 5. APATITE: Apatite is another mineral that forms beautiful crystals of many different colors. Some of these colors are white, brown, green, violet, blue and yellow. Yellow is the most common color.

You can scratch apatite with a knife, too. Apatite in turn will scratch any of the hardness minerals below it. Apatite, like each of the other minerals, is able to scratch itself.

FELDSPAR

Number 6. FELDSPAR: Feldspar is about the most common mineral on the earth. When this mineral breaks up and rots, it turns into clay. Clay is found almost everywhere.

Your knife will not scratch feldspar, but the feldspar will scratch your knife!

QUARTZ

Number 7. QUARTZ: Quartz is a common mineral you have already read about. It comes in many colors. A beautiful kind of quartz is named Tiger's Eye and is used in jewelry.

Quartz sand is melted and turned into clear glass. Radios and phonographs very often have special quartz crystals in them. Quartz is very useful. It is the hardest mineral you are apt to find easily.

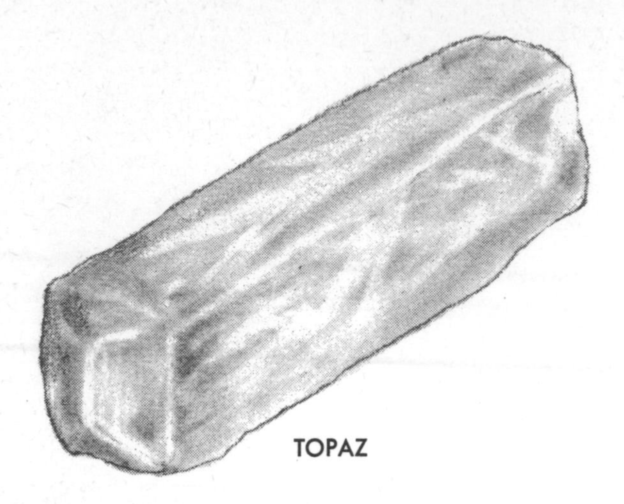

TOPAZ

Number 8. TOPAZ: Topaz is a very hard stone. It will scratch quartz or any of the other minerals below quartz. Topaz is prized as a gem stone because it is very beautiful. This stone is commonly yellow.

CORUNDUM (ruby)

Number 9. CORUNDUM: Corundum is next to the hardest mineral. Some crystals of this mineral are also gem stones. Ruby is a clear red corundum crystal. Such a crystal is quite valuable.

Ordinary corundum is crushed into small bits and made into sandpaper.

Number 10. DIAMOND: This is the hardest mineral known on earth. Nothing is harder than diamond. It is many times as hard as corundum. Clear crystals are made into jewels. Dark-colored diamonds are used to polish and cut other hard stones, as well as other diamonds, too. Diamonds are valuable because they are very hard, beautiful and rare.

These are the hardness minerals. They are all used for many things. Testing the hardness of other minerals is just one of the things for which they are used.

As you become more interested in rocks and minerals, you will want to have a set of hardness testing minerals. A set is not expensive, for most sets do not contain a diamond. Since a diamond could only test another diamond, there is little need for one in the set.

Even before you have such a set, many tests can be made with your fingernail, a penny, a pocket knife and a piece of quartz.

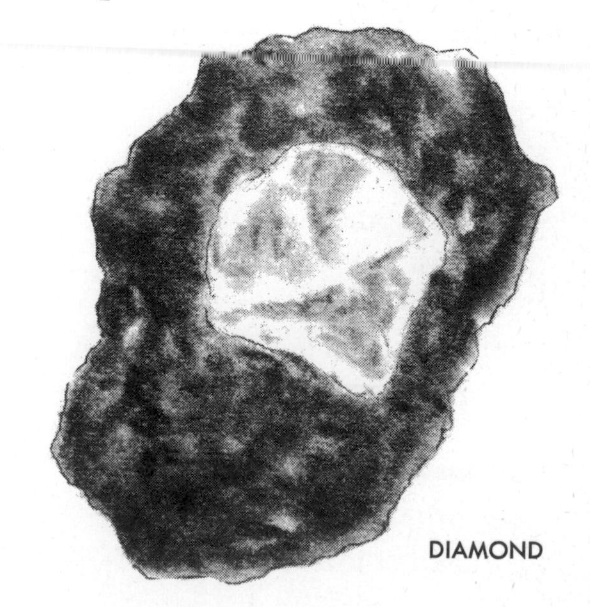

DIAMOND

SIMPLE TESTS

How can you tell what kind of rock it is?

YOU CAN test for the name of a rock or mineral with a streak plate. A streak plate is made of unglazed tile.

Many specimens leave a colored streak when they are rubbed on the streak plate. The color of the streak helps to name the rock. You can make red, blue, black and many other colored streaks. Some samples will not even make a streak!

RUB THE ROCK OR THE MINERAL ON A STREAK PLATE.

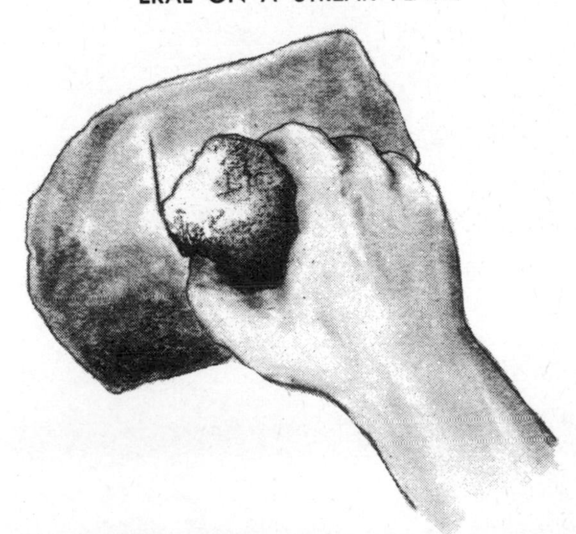

THE STREAKS MADE BY THE HARDNESS MINERALS VARY FROM WHITE TO GRAY, WHILE SOME OF THE MINERALS MAKE NO STREAKS OR ARE COLORLESS. GENERALLY, NON-METALLIC MINERALS MAKE COLORLESS TO LIGHT GRAY STREAKS, AND METALLIC MINERALS MAKE DARK GRAY TO BLACK STREAKS.

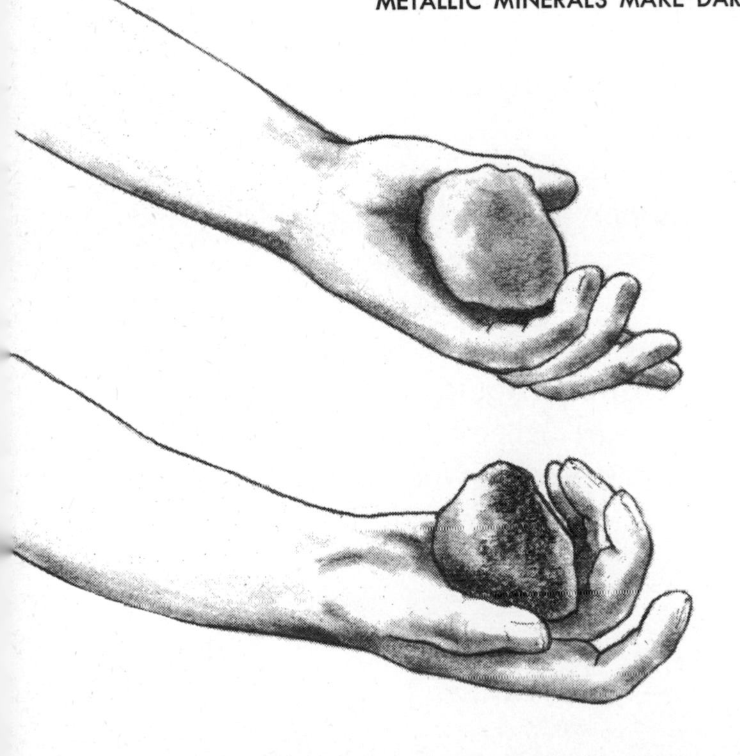

A SIMPLE WAY TO TEST ROCKS AND MINERALS FOR WEIGHT IS TO HOLD A DIFFERENT SPECIMEN IN EACH HAND. EVEN THOUGH BOTH ROCKS ARE OF THE SAME SIZE, ONE WILL WEIGH MORE THAN THE OTHER.

How can you test a rock or mineral for weight?

YOU CANNOT look at a rock or mineral and tell how heavy it is. Yet, some minerals or rocks are much heavier than others. When you pick up a sample rock, you can tell if it seems heavy or light.

When you try this with a different rock in each hand, you can tell which is the heavier. Both samples must be about the same size, of course. You will be surprised to see how easily you can tell the difference in weight between two rocks. Whether the rock is heavy or light may help to tell its name.

More advanced books will show you other ways of finding the weight of a rock or mineral.

FOSSILS

What is a fossil?

A FOSSIL is the remains of some animal or plant which is no longer living. It has been dead for many years and only part of the animal or plant is left today. This part is called a fossil.

Clams often turn into fossils. Here is how this can happen.

When a clam dies, the soft parts of its body soon rot away. But the shell of the clam is very hard. It is made of calcium, like our bones, and cannot rot away. The shell sinks to the sand at the bottom of the sea.

Many years pass and other shells join the first shell. Fine sand washes over the shells and buries them. In time the sand changes into sandstone. But the shells are still there, buried with the sandstone.

Millions of years go by and the sea bottom becomes dry land. The sandstone can now be seen.

If you should dig down into the sandstone, you would find the old clam shells. You would call them fossils now. They are called that because fossils are hardened traces of animals or plants which have been preserved in the earth.

HERE ARE CLAM SHELL FOSSILS WHICH HAVE BEEN PRESERVED IN SANDSTONE.

THE WORD *FOSSIL* COMES FROM A LATIN WORD MEANING "DUG UP." THE DISCOVERY OF FOSSIL REMAINS OF ANIMALS ON LAND AND IN THE SEA HAS GIVEN SCIENTISTS MUCH INFORMATION ABOUT THE WORLD AS IT WAS MILLIONS OF YEARS AGO.

Why do we study fossils?

SOME day you may find a fossil. You will want to know its name. You may ask yourself, "Where did this come from? Is it an animal or is it a rock? How did it get here? Is it valuable?" These and many other questions may occur to you.

The scientists who search for fossils and study them are known as *paleontologists*. By learning of life and changes that occurred on earth in the past, they can supply answers for the future.

Fossils give us a record and a picture of the past that is beyond the ken of human memory. From them we can find out not only what certain plants and animals looked like, but can deduce other things. For example, by finding fossil shellfish in presently mountainous regions, we can scientifically conclude that the area was once under sea water. By finding fossils of tropical plants in Greenland, we must conclude that this land mass once had a climate quite different from what it has today.

Where are fossils found?

ONE of the best places to look for fossils is in sedimentary rocks. Soft shale and sandstone often have fossils in them. These are both sedimentary rocks.

Limestone is a sedimentary rock made up of millions of tiny shells of sea animals. Sometimes the shells of the animals can be seen in the limestone. You could think of this kind of limestone as "fossil stone."

THE SHELLS OF SEA ANIMALS CONTRIBUTE TO THE FORMATION OF LIMESTONE. LIMESTONE IS, THEREFORE, A GOOD SOURCE OF FOSSILS. NOTE THE SHELLS IN THIS STONE.

GOOD EXAMPLES OF PETRIFIED WOOD MAY BE FOUND IN THE PETRIFIED FOREST NATIONAL PARK IN THE STATE OF ARIZONA.

Trees and plants that are near lakes and streams often fall into the water. Sometimes they sink to the bottom and are buried in the soft mud. The years pass by. More mud covers the old trees. Slowly the trees change into fossils.

This takes many years to occur. But finally the tree has been changed from wood into a mineral. It is no longer made of wood, but of stone. We call this kind of stone petrified wood.

There are places in the West where whole forests of petrified trees or fossils are found. Some areas have been set aside as national or state monuments to preserve these trees and fossils from souvenir hunters. You may some day visit one of these places yourself.

RARE STONES

What makes a mineral a gem stone?

GEM stones are rare and more difficult to find than ordinary rocks. They are harder to find because there are not so many of them. If a stone is hard to find, if it is beautiful, and if it can be polished, it then becomes valuable. This kind of stone is named a gem stone.

For hundreds of years men have looked for valuable gem stones and minerals. Today other men are still hunting for new places to find gem stones.

A ruby is a beautiful red-colored gem stone. When a ruby is polished, it sparkles and shines. The color of the ruby helps to make it valuable.

Other gem stones are opals, pearls, emeralds and diamonds. Emeralds and diamonds are the most expensive and rarest gem stones. All gem stones are beautiful. Gem stones are used in jewelry. They are often set in rings.

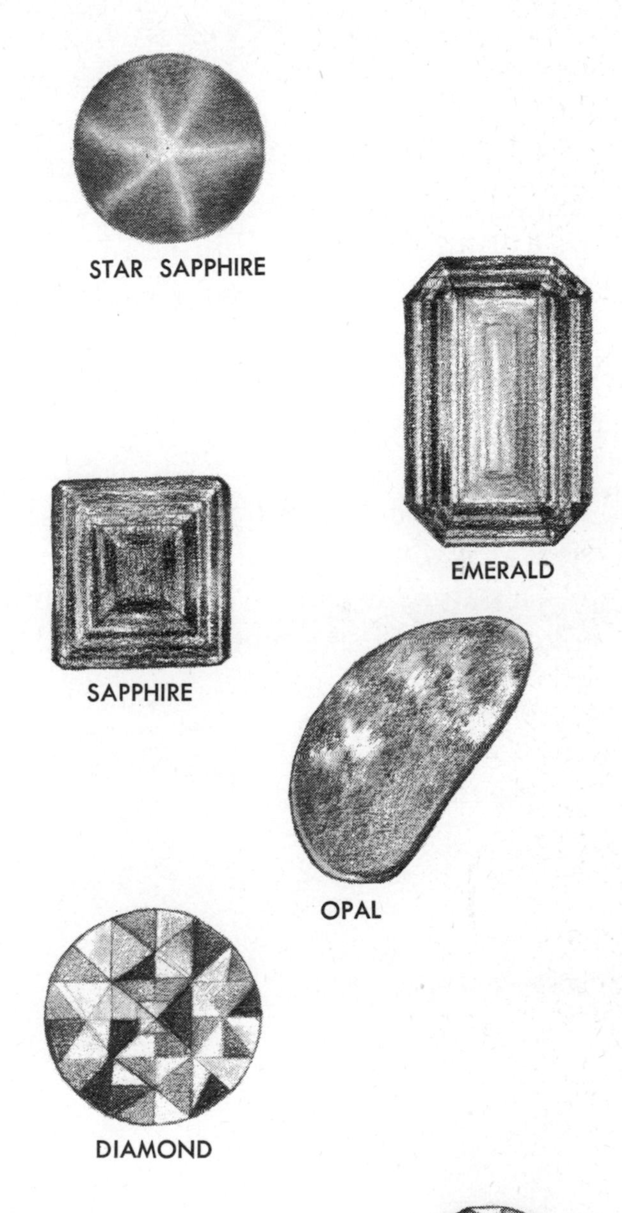

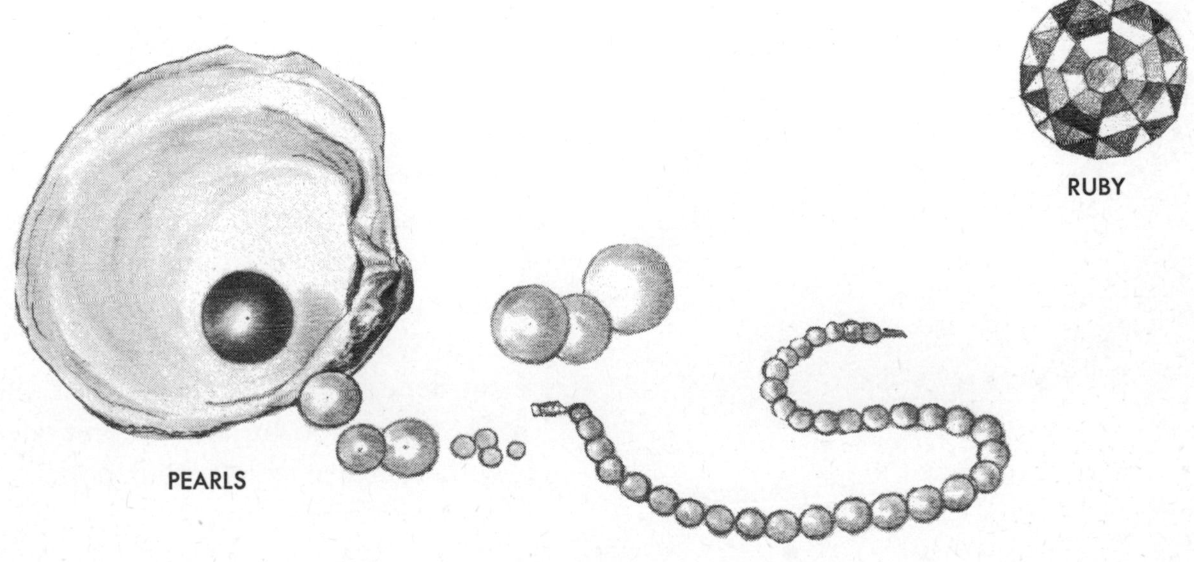

PUMICE

What is pumice?

PUMICE is an igneous rock. It is made by volcanoes. Sometimes the volcano throws out gobs of molten rock. Little holes grow in the rock before it cools. These holes are caused by steam or gas trapped in the molten rock. The holes in pumice look just like the holes in a loaf of bread!

Pumice is a stone that can float on water! It floats on water because it is so very light.

This stone is used to polish fine furniture and to make building materials.

PUMICE

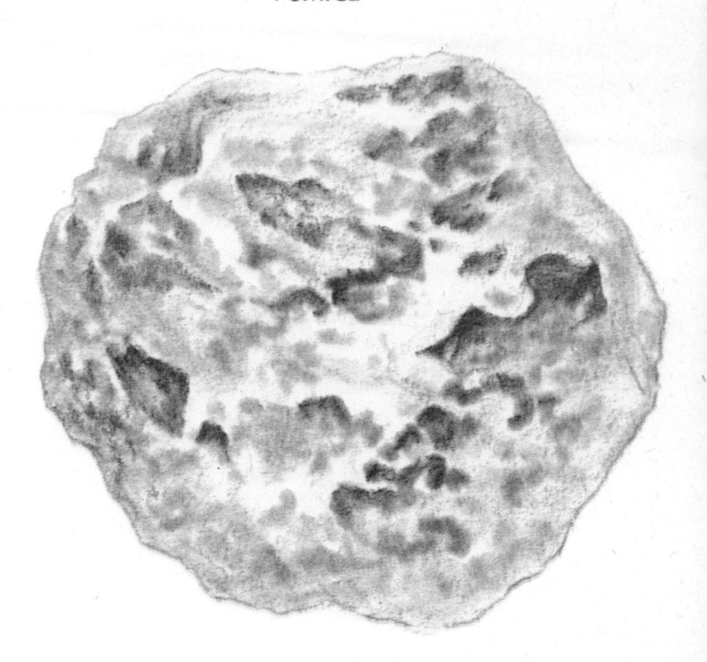

COAL

COAL

What is coal?

COAL IS A sedimentary rock that will burn. Coal burns just as wood does. It is used to build warm fires.

Coal was made millions of years ago. This rock is made from plants, and trees or ferns that lived long ago.

These trees and plants became buried just like fossils. In time they turned into coal. Coal is really the remains of many trees and plants. You can think of coal as "fossil wood."

Coal deposits are found all over the United States. The largest and best ones are in the eastern part of our country.

ICE

ICE

What is ice?

ICE IS THE colorless mineral that floats in water! Ice is really a water crystal, formed when the temperature of water or moisture in the air reaches the *freezing point,* indicated by 32° on the Fahrenheit thermometer or 0° on the centigrade thermometer.

Ice expands (increases its volume) as it forms. If one were to measure out eleven equal parts of water and freeze it, one would find that it takes up as much space as twelve parts. When there is no room for water to expand, pressure becomes strong — water pipes, for example, will often split open in winter.

Icebergs, being lighter than water, will float. In the sea about one-eighth of an iceberg is visible — the rest of it is hidden below the surface.

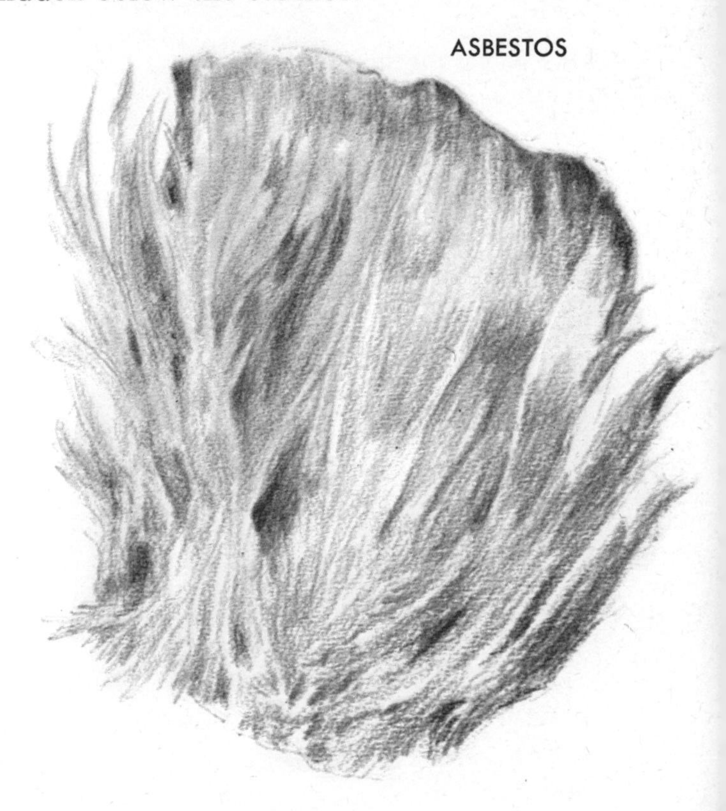
ASBESTOS

ASBESTOS

What is asbestos?

ASBESTOS is a mineral that does not burn! It is useful around stoves and hot places, for it will keep things near the stove from burning.

Asbestos is a light-colored mineral that comes from a kind of serpentine. It is made into asbestos cloth, asbestos paper and other helpful things. If you wore a pair of asbestos gloves, you could touch and handle hot things without getting burned!

START A ROCK AND MINERAL COLLECTION

How do you begin a rock and mineral collection?

YOU will find it easy to start a rock and mineral collection. Begin to collect by looking near your home.

If you have a garden, you may find a rock there. If there is an open field close by, it should contain some rocks you will want to have in your collection.

Are workmen building a new house near your home? They may have dug up some rocks or minerals you do not have. Sometimes the builders bring in new kinds of rocks. Look them over. There might be some you will want to collect, but ask permission first.

If you go into the country, watch for other new rocks or minerals. Look at new road cuts. This is often a good place to collect rocks. A dry creek or stream is another excellent place to look.

One of the finest places will be in a rock quarry. Here you are sure to find some worthwhile specimens. Of course, you must be careful to watch out for overhanging rocks or loose stones. It is well to collect with a partner — and more fun, too!

What will you need to collect rocks and minerals?

YOU WILL need something to put your specimens in when you find them. If you are collecting near home, a heavy paper bag will do. But put in only a few small rocks at a time.

Most collectors use a collecting bag made of strong cloth. It has a strap that goes over your shoulder to help carry heavy loads. Surplus goods stores usually have a bag of this kind.

You will often need to break off rocks and break open new ones. A hammer or even another stone will sometimes help. With a hammer, or a prospector's pick, you can chip off a small piece of rock from a larger one.

Rock and mineral collectors like to take home only one or two of each kind of rock they find. It does not help to take too many of each. You would soon run out of room in which to keep them.

How can you keep your rocks and minerals?

YOU WILL want to keep your best rocks and minerals. It will help if you keep each kind together. The igneous rocks can go into one box. All of the sedimentary and the metamorphic rocks should be put into other boxes.

Shoe boxes or wooden cigar boxes make good containers. A label on the outside of the box will help you to locate specimens quickly.

Each rock should be labeled separately before you put it into your collection bag. A good system is to put a piece of adhesive tape with a number on it on the sample. In your collecting notebook write the name of the specimen and where you found it. Later on, at home, paint a small round white spot on your specimen with white paint. India ink numbers over the white paint will show up fine.

Start your numbers with one, two, three, and so on. This will help you to keep your collection organized. Do not carelessly try to collect everything and put off labeling your rocks until later.

IDENTIFICATION CHART OF MAJOR SPECIMENS

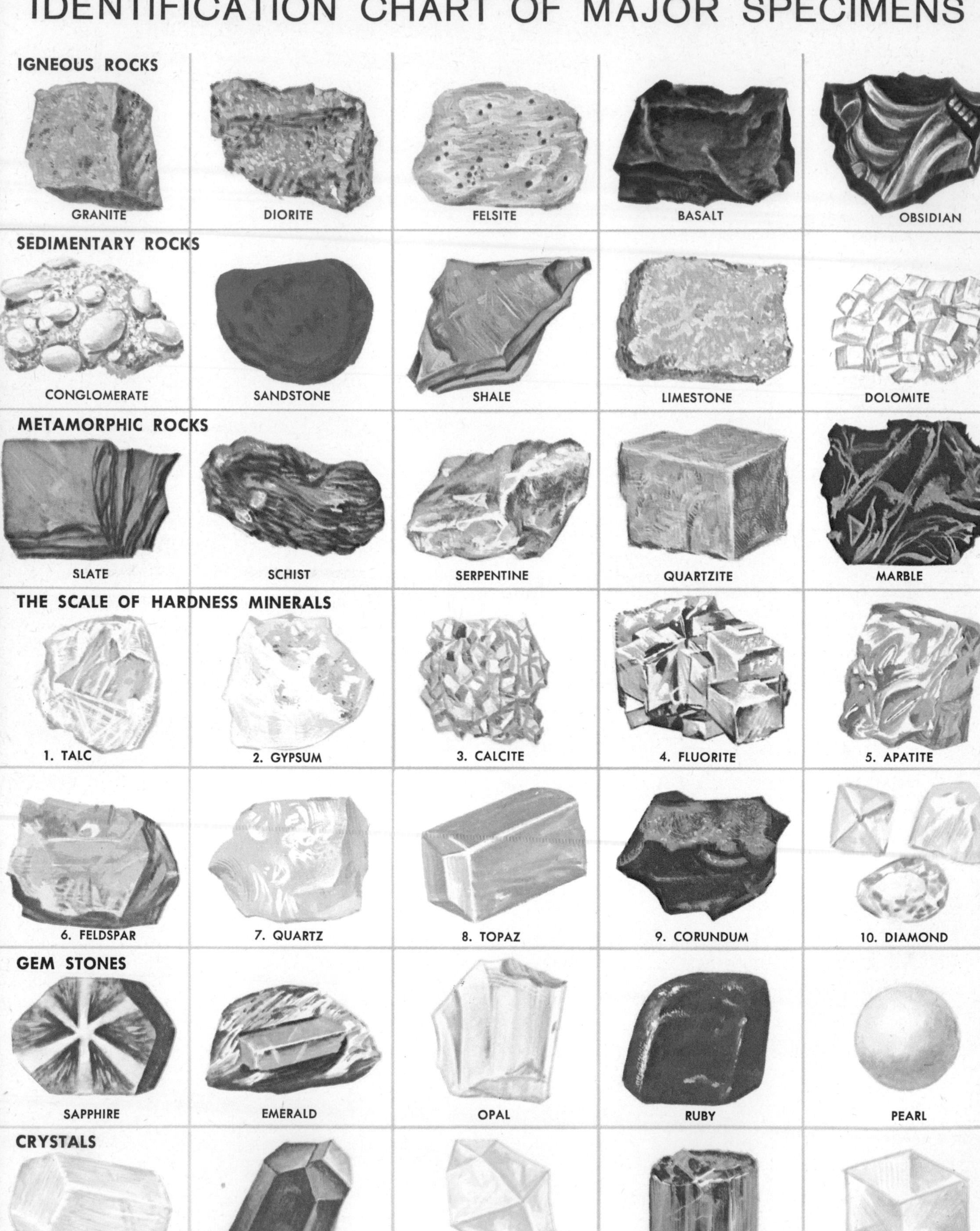

THE HOW AND WHY WONDER BOOK OF WEATHER

By George Bonsall
Illustrated by George Pay

Edited under the supervision of
Dr. Paul E. Blackwood
Washington, D. C.

Text and illustrations approved by

Oakes A. White
Brooklyn Children's Museum
Brooklyn, New York

GROSSET & DUNLAP • Publishers • NEW YORK

INTRODUCTION

This *How and Why Wonder Book* deals with a subject that is important to everyone, for in many ways weather rules the life of man. And like the others in the *How and Why Wonder Book* series, this one answers dozens of basic questions about an area of knowledge in which scientists are constantly exploring. So this book is of interest to science-minded children and their parents. It explains how air, sun and water intermingle in a thousand different ways to produce an ever-changing yet predictable weather pattern.

The *How and Why Wonder Books* not only give accurate information about scientific subjects, but they also explain the various ways in which scientists explore and investigate the universe. The experiment is one of these ways. And this book emphasizes experiments. It suggests dozens of simple activities which young readers will want to try. Doing the experiments is a way of practicing one of the most important methods used by scientists to get accurate information about the environment.

If you have ever wondered about snow or fog, hurricanes or tornadoes, the seasons, or any other topic concerning weather, you will find much helpful information and colorful pictures in these pages.

Paul E. Blackwood

Dr. Blackwood is a professional employee in the U. S. Office of Education. This book was edited by him in his private capacity and no official support or endorsement by the Office of Education is intended or should be inferred.

Library of Congress Catalog Card Number: 61-1550

1971 Printing

CONTENTS

WEATHER

One of the seasons is spring, which usually includes the months of March, April and May. Rainy weather occurs often in the spring, a time of the year when plants and crops begin to grow.

What makes weather?

WHY DOES the earth have a variety of seasons and climate, while the moon does not? The answer is — weather.

Clouds, wind, rain and snow — these are some of the things we can see or feel as signs of what we call weather.

You may have sometimes wondered why it is that weather conditions are constantly changing. Wind, temperature, air pressure and moisture are the factors responsible. When air moves from place to place at varying rates of speed, we call it the wind. As it moves, it may carry warm air, cool air, dry air or moist air. Air temperature really affects weather more than anything else, and this is largely determined by the sun. (The sun sends its energy into our atmosphere, where it is absorbed and transformed into heat.) High-pressure areas, created by cold air, generally indicate fair weather. Low-pressure areas are created by warm air (which weighs less than cold air) and generally indicate cloudy or stormy weather. Moving air (winds) usually follows a route going from a high-pressure area to a low-pressure area. Moisture in the air is simply water vapor, but it may take the form of rain, sleet, snow, fog, clouds or measurable humidity.

Sun + Air + Water = Weather

Summer is the warmest season of the year. It is a time when the sun shines most directly over the land. In the United States, summer includes the months of June, July and August, a time of the year when many people go to the seashore.

The season between summer and winter is autumn. It includes the months of September, October and November. It is the time of year when leaves fall from the trees, and so autumn is often called fall.

Winter is the coldest season of the year. In the United States, it includes the months of December, January and February, a time of the year when children like to ice-skate, go sledding and play in the snow.

Is there weather on the moon?

But the moon is lighted and warmed by the sun. Why doesn't the moon have clouds and rain and wind and snow? The moon has neither air nor water, so there can be no weather on the moon.

THE AIR ON TOP OF YOUR HEAD

Can you see air?

WHAT do you know about this ocean of air you live in? Do you breathe it? Can you see through it? Do you feel it when it moves? The answer is yes. But it's hard to picture something you can't see. It's hard to believe something is real if you can't look at it and touch it. Are there ways of showing that air is real?

When you turn a glass upside down and push it into water, no water will go into the glass. The air in the glass keeps the water from coming in, which shows that air takes up space.

Does air take up space?

You might try turning a glass upside down and pushing it straight down into a bowl of water. There is something which keeps the water from filling the glass — isn't there? You thought the glass was empty. It wasn't filled with something to drink, but it was full. The glass was full of air. Only real things take up space. Air and water can't fit into the same glass any more than you and a friend can fit into the same clothes at the same time. The water can't get in the glass unless you tilt it to one side and let some of the air out.

Is air real?

Next try blowing up a balloon. When you pinch it, what do you feel inside? The only thing you put into the balloon was air. It must be air that you feel. If you feel the air, then the air is there. The air is real.

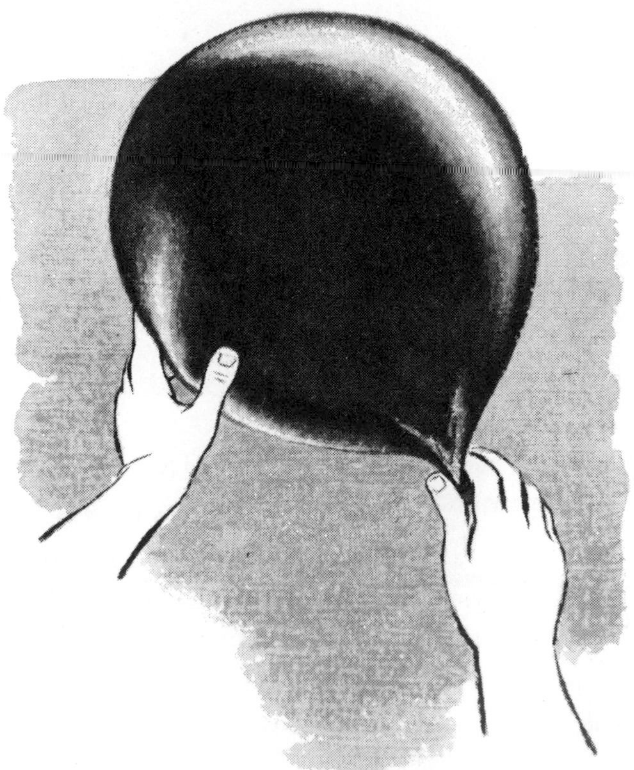

You can actually feel air by pressing on a blown-up balloon. This shows that air is real.

Is air heavy?

How much does air weigh? It depends on when and where you measure it. The air in your living room may weigh as much as you do. Right now there is a column of air resting on your head and shoulders which is several hundred miles high. It weighs hundreds of pounds. How can you support such a weight? You couldn't bear it at all if the same air pressure in your body didn't also push in the opposite direction. The experiment described below, and illustrated on the right, helps to explain this idea.

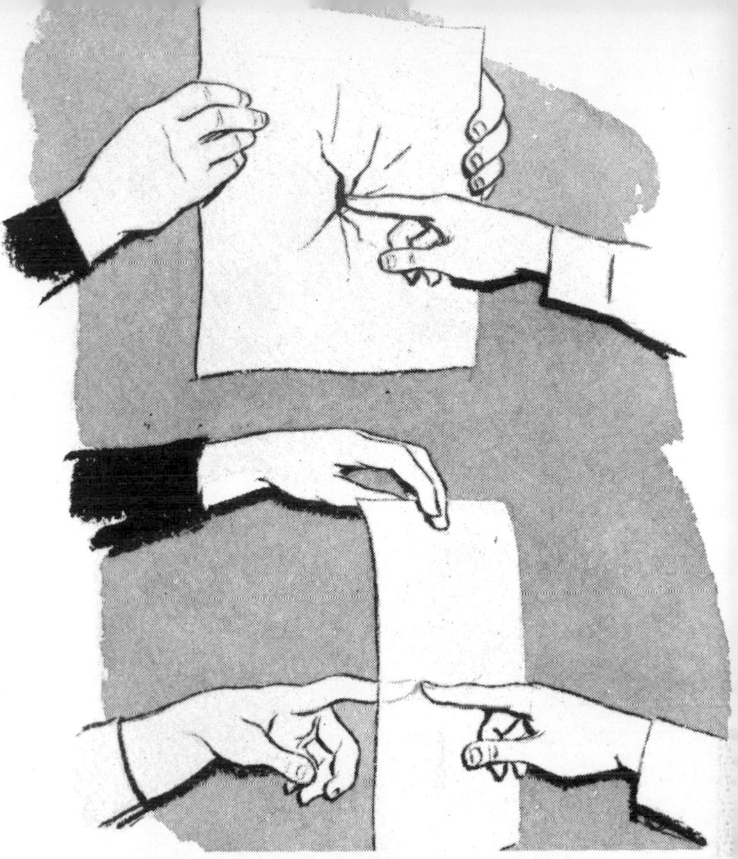

Air has weight and presses down on us. However, the pressure in our bodies is equal to the air pressing down on us, so we don't feel the weight of the air.

Does air push in all directions?

Ask someone to hold a thin piece of paper in both hands. Now push your finger against one side of the paper. You've poked a hole right through. Take another piece of paper. This time use a finger on each hand. Push at the same spot from each side of the paper. Nothing happens. The pressure is equal on both sides of the paper. So, too, the pressure of air in your body is equal to the pressure of that column of air resting on your head and shoulders.

You can squeeze air, as this experiment with a hand pump shows.

Can you squeeze water?

The tall column of air presses down on your head the way a tall column of water presses down on a deep-sea diver. But there is one big difference between these columns. You cannot squeeze water.

Can you squeeze air?

But you squeeze air every time you use a pump to blow up a basketball. If you held your finger over the end of the pump, it would be harder to push the handle, but you could at least push it part way.

AIR PRESSES DOWN

Does air press down?

SUPPOSE you had a stack of pancakes three feet high. Each of the pancakes weighs something. Each is pressed down by the total weight of all the pancakes on top of it. The bottom pancakes would be squeezed the most. The top pancakes would be squeezed the least. But you would get more to eat if you took a two-inch stack of pancakes from the bottom of the pile than you would if you helped yourself to a two-inch stack from the top. Air is like these pancakes.

Air is made up of tiny bits called molecules. More than a *trillion* of these molecules could fit in a space the size of the head of a pin! They squeeze one another like the stack of pancakes, so the greatest number of molecules is found in a layer very close to the earth.

Helium is used to inflate balloons and airships, which then rise in the air. The higher up you go, the thinner and lighter is the air.

Is air lighter on a mountain or in a valley ?

Up in the mountains and high in the sky, the air becomes thinner. The molecules are farther apart. (The pancakes were farther apart on top of the stack.) Way up high, the air is so thin that mountain climbers and pilots must wear oxygen masks to breathe.

You have seen balloons filled with a gas called helium. Helium is much lighter than air. When the lighter-than-air balloon leaves the ground, it rises through the thick layer of air like a cork rising in a tank of water. But the balloon cannot keep rising forever. After it has risen a few miles, the air becomes so light and thin that the balloon is no longer lighter than the air.

Why is it colder on a mountain than in a valley?

Something else happens when you climb high mountains or fly in the sky. You get colder. There are many mountains in the world which have snow on their peaks all year round. This is because our ocean of air is graduated from heavy layers to very thin layers as we get farther from sea level. High up the air is thinner, lighter and colder because molecules are farther apart.

If you were to take temperature readings of the air as you climbed a mountain, you would find that the higher you went, the colder it would get.

Does rubbing make things hotter?

Close to earth the molecules are all squeezed together. They are restless. They push and shove harder and harder. As they rub against one another they become hotter. So it is possible for you to see two different effects of air pressure in the same part of the country — snow on a mountaintop, where the air is thin and molecules are far apart, and flowers growing in a warm valley beneath, where molecules of air have been squeezed tightly together and heated up.

Feel the molecules which make up your skin become hotter when you rub your palms together very quickly.

Feel the side of a hand pump just after it has been used. It is warm. The molecules have been squeezed together.

HEATING BY DAY—COOLING BY NIGHT

Dark-colored things hold on to heat from the sun's rays better than light-colored things. For this reason, many people wear white garments in the summertime, since white absorbs less heat from the sun than darker colors.

Why do you wear light-colored clothing in summer?

IN THE winter you wear warm clothes to protect you from the cold. Most of these clothes are dark-colored — dark reds, navy blues, deep greens. In the summer, when you wear fewer clothes, these clothes are often of white or pale colors. Why? The answer is in the sun's rays.

Try putting a piece of white paper in the sun. Next to it put a piece of black paper. After a few minutes the black paper will feel warmer than the white paper. Things which are dark-colored absorb more of the sun's rays and produce more heat than light-colored things. The dark clothing keeps you warmer in the winter time. It holds on to the heat from the sun's rays. The light-colored clothing you wear in summer helps keep you cool. It does not absorb as much heat from the sun.

If you put the piece of black paper in the sun again and feel it two minutes later, five minutes later, and ten minutes later, you can feel it getting warmer. It gets warmer because the sun shines on it for a longer time. Your skin feels the same way the longer you lie out in the sun. It gets warmer and warmer.

When does the earth cool off best?

The same thing that happens to you in the sun happens to the rocks and soil and water on earth. The longer the sun's rays shine upon them, the hotter they become. The earth grows warmer by day. At night, when the sun is gone, the earth cools off.

WINTER

EACH of the four seasons in our northern hemisphere wears its own face. So it is as easy to tell them apart as it is for you to recognize each of your friends. Each season has its own weather. Each weather change makes a change in you. How does winter's face look? How can you tell when the winter season is coming?

Is a winter day longer or shorter than a winter night?

The days grow much shorter and the nights grow very long. The wind blows colder. The sun doesn't seem to be as warm. The season is changing. You're changing, too. You're changing into heavier clothes which protect you from the cold. You're changing the games you play and the food you eat. You're beginning to spend more time indoors. What happens when winter finally comes?

In winter the days are shorter and the nights are longer than at any other time of year. The sun rises later, after you are up and dressed. It sets at night before suppertime. The soil and the rocks and the water are warmed by the sun during the short day and have much time to cool during the long night.

During the summer, the sun's rays shine directly down. In the winter, the rays are slanted.

Why do the sun's rays give less heat in winter?

Even when the sun is shining, it does not heat the soil and the rocks and the water during the winter months as much as it does at other times of the year. As you watch the sun cross the sky, you'll notice that it is not as high as at other seasons of the year. The position of the sun in the winter sky causes the sun's rays to strike the earth at a slant.

If you pretend that a flashlight is the sun and shine it down on a table at a slant, you will see that the light is spread over a much larger area than it is when you shine the flashlight straight down. The sun's light hits the earth at a wide slant during the winter. It is spread over a wider area and does not give as much heat as it does when its rays shine straight down.

SPRING

JUST as you are beginning to feel that winter will never end, things begin to happen which tell you it will. A warm breeze blows across an open field. Large cracks appear in the ice on the skating pond. Rivers and streams swell and overflow with melting snow. Changes happen to you, too. You take off the extra sweaters under your coat. Your nose and hands and feet don't get as cold when you play outside. You spend more time outdoors. All these signs and changes mean something. Spring is coming!

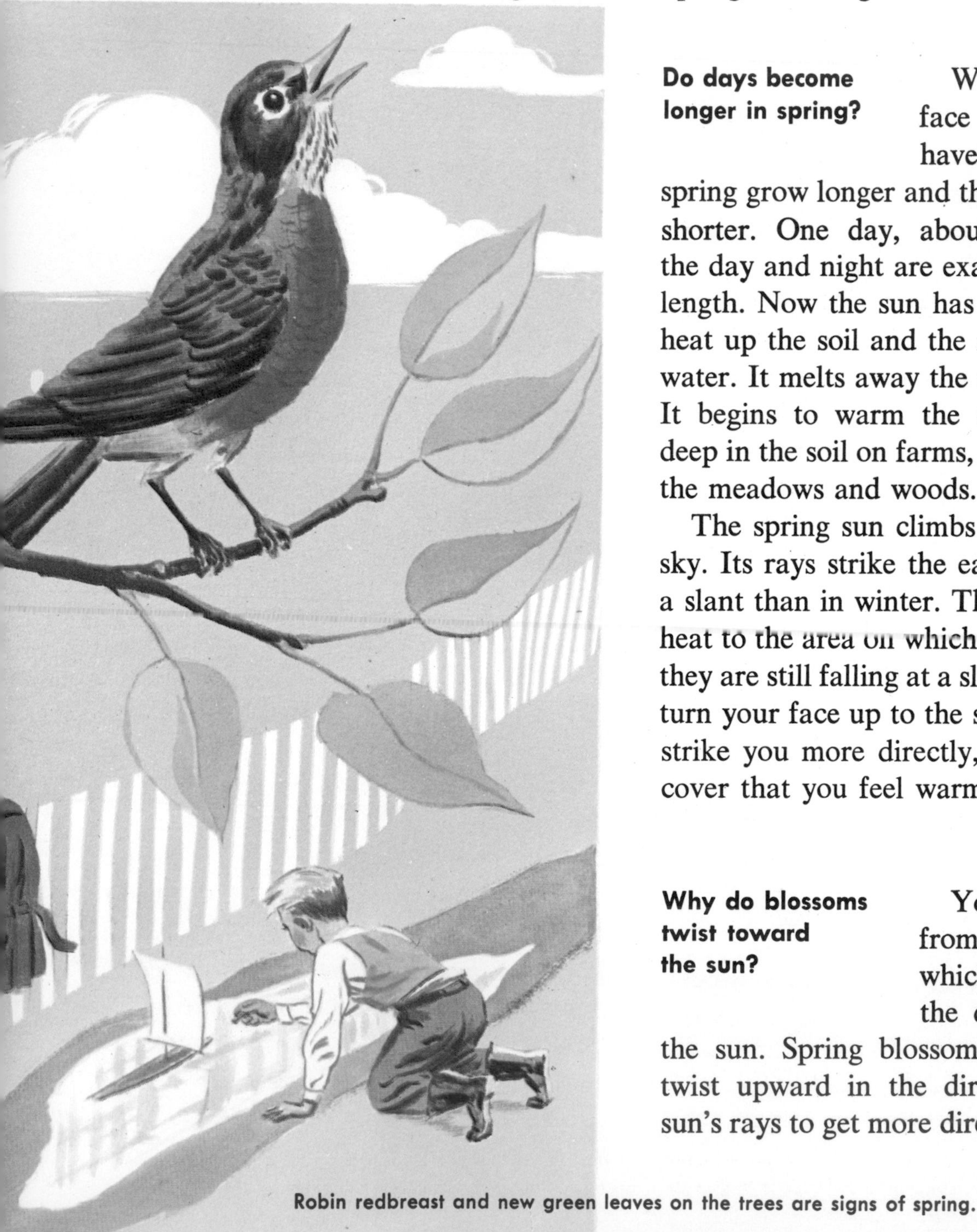

Do days become longer in spring?

What sort of face does spring have? The days of spring grow longer and the nights grow shorter. One day, about March 21, the day and night are exactly the same length. Now the sun has more time to heat up the soil and the rocks and the water. It melts away the snow and ice. It begins to warm the seeds planted deep in the soil on farms, in gardens, in the meadows and woods.

The spring sun climbs higher in the sky. Its rays strike the earth at less of a slant than in winter. They give more heat to the area on which they fall. But they are still falling at a slant and if you turn your face up to the sun so its rays strike you more directly, you will discover that you feel warmer.

Why do blossoms twist toward the sun?

You learned this from the flowers which turn during the day to follow the sun. Spring blossoms stretch and twist upward in the direction of the sun's rays to get more direct heat.

Robin redbreast and new green leaves on the trees are signs of spring.

SUMMER

When do we have our longest days and shortest nights?

SOMETIMES so quietly you hardly know it has come, summer arrives. Just as winter and spring have their signals, so summer has its signals. What do you see when you look for the face of summer?

You see that the days are longer than at any other time of year. The sun shines in your eyes in the morning and wakes you up. It sets long after supper and the nights are short.

You take off jackets and heavy socks and put on light clothing. You eat more cold foods and drink cool drinks. You enjoy games that you can only enjoy in the hot weather. You swim outdoors and you go boating.

Summer is here!

In the summer, the path of the sun is longer and farther to the north than the sun's winter path. The path of the sun on June 22 is longer than on any other day, which makes June 22 the longest day in the year.

Does the summer sun rise high?

What happens to our sun in the summer? It crosses the sky higher than at any other time of the year. Its rays bring more heat to the earth. They are direct rays and shine on a smaller area. These rays strike the earth for more hours each day. The short nights of summer mean less time for the earth to cool before the sun rises and begins its job of heating all over again the next day.

You can understand from the experiment pictured here one reason why the earth grows so warm in summer. Two pieces of black paper have been cut the same size, with pieces of cardboard placed behind them to keep them stiff. One piece is laid flat on the ground so that the sun shines on it directly. The other is propped up so that the sun strikes it at a slant. After a few minutes the black paper which is flat on the ground becomes warmer than the piece which is propped up. In the same way, the earth is made warmer by the summer sun's more direct rays than by the more slanting rays of the other seasons. You might try this experiment yourself, though it may be hard to tell the difference in temperature unless conditions are ideal.

The rocks and the soil and the water on earth, like the paper you placed in the sun, are being heated for a longer time during the long summer days. They become hotter and hotter.

In the summer, direct rays of the sun strike the earth. This experiment will show that the earth is made warmer by direct rays than by the slanted rays of the sun in other seasons of the year.

In the fall, the path of the sun across the sky becomes shorter than it was in the summer. The days become shorter and the nights become longer. Note the sun's journey across the sky.

FALL

Do days get shorter in the fall?

ONE DAY, in September, you will notice that the days are getting a little cooler. The winds are brisk. You put on a sweater when you go out to play. After a summer of salads and cool drinks, you enjoy eating a bowl of hot soup. Is it your imagination or is the sun setting a little earlier? It isn't your imagination. The sun is beginning to make a shorter journey across the sky each day. There are fewer hours of heating. The nights grow a little longer. There are more hours of cooling. You can see that the sun is not quite so high in the sky as it was in summer. The sun's rays strike the earth at more of a slant and lose some of their heating power.

About September 21, there comes another date when the length of the day is exactly the same as the length of the night.

Soon you notice the leaves of the trees changing colors and falling to the ground. They blow about in the wind. The flowers and fruits and vegetables of summer are gone. This is the face of fall.

What causes changes in seasons?

You have lived through four seasons, four different weather patterns, four changes in the way you dress, the games you play, sometimes even the kind of house you live in. All these changes were made because of the weather.

Are you ready to start another year? Will you know when winter is coming?

HOTTER IS FASTER

This experiment, using talcum powder and an electric light bulb, shows that hot air rises. When air is heated, it expands and gets lighter.

Does hot air rise?

WHAT happens when air is heated?

An electric light bulb which has been burning a few minutes heats the air above it and causes that air to rise. If you sprinkle a tiny amount of talcum powder or corn starch into the air a few inches above the bulb, you can watch as the powdered air is pushed upward.

Have you ever watched a coal-burning fire? If there is no strong current of air, smoke goes straight up. What we see are bits of black carbon, which will settle down later as soot. Smoke rises because the air has been heated. Hot air is lighter than cold air. It rises like the lighter-than-air balloon.

What happens to air when it is heated?

Something else happens when air is heated. The tiny particles, or molecules of which air is made, begin to move about faster and faster. As they bump one another harder and harder, they move farther apart. They take up more room. You can watch this happen. Measure around the largest part of a balloon with a tape measure or piece of thread. Then place the balloon in the bright sun. After a few minutes, measure it again and you will see that the balloon is larger. It has the same weight of air inside, but it takes up more space. So we know that air which is heated not only rises, but it also expands.

AN AIR EXCHANGE

Does cold air move?

A HOT radiator is a good thing to stir up the air molecules. As the air near the radiator is heated, it rises. Cold air sweeps in to take its place. This cold air is heated by the radiator and it rises. More cold air rushes in. This is how air keeps moving or circulating about in the room. The warm air is pushed away by the cold air. When the cold air becomes warm, it rises and more cold air moves in. This goes on and on, around and around, indefinitely.

Where is the warmest part of a room?

So you would expect to find the temperature of the room higher near the ceiling than near the floor. If you let fresh air into the room by opening the window both top and bottom, the cool air coming in at the bottom will push warm air out at the top.

You can watch this happen. Fasten paper strips to parts of a window, as shown in the illustration. Watch the directions in which the air moves the paper strips. The strips at the top will move out as warm air is pushed out. The strips at the bottom will move in as cold air rushes in.

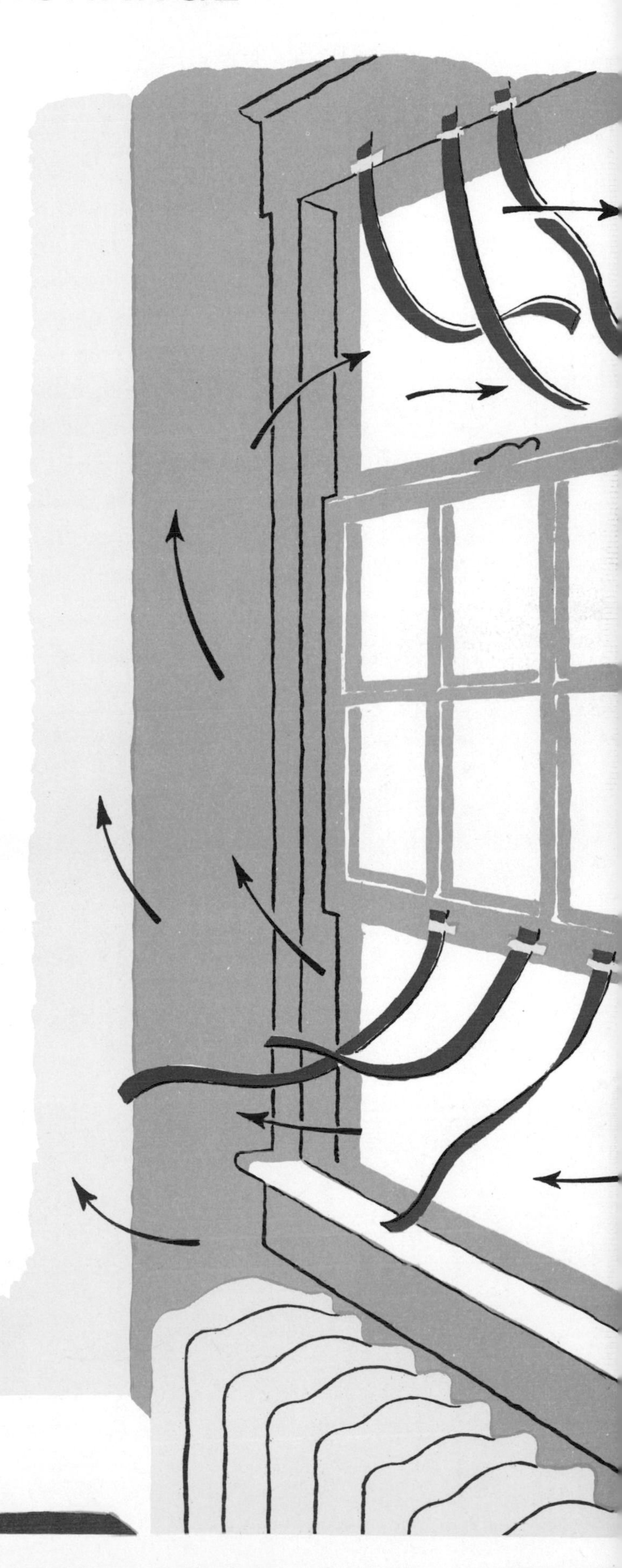

Warm air rises, but as it rises, it is replaced by cooler air. This experiment, using paper strips fastened to parts of a window, shows this idea.

A TINY TORNADO

Does the earth heat evenly?

AIR circulates in the room because of a difference in temperature. Winds blow outdoors for the same reason. All day long the rays of the sun shoot through space and through the earth's ocean of air, striking the soil, rocks and water. As the soil, rocks and water are heated, they heat the layer of air nearest to them. Do they heat it evenly? No. By placing black and white papers in the sun, you showed that darker materials heat faster than lighter materials.

When does air move fastest?

Some areas of the earth are lighter than others and will absorb fewer of the sun's rays. Asphalt is dark, so a hot asphalt driveway will make the air above it very warm. As the warm air rises, the cool air from a shady spot next to it will rush in to take its place. As the air rushes in quickly, it will pick up leaves and papers in its path and whirl them about like a top. What is happening is a miniature version of a violent storm called a tornado. The greater the difference in temperature, the quicker the air will move.

This picture-diagram shows, on a very small scale, how a tornado takes place. Warm air rises; cold air comes in to take its place. As the cold air moves in, it picks up objects in its path and whirls them about as a tornado might do.

WHY BREEZES BLOW

Why does wind blow?

SOIL and rock heat much faster than water. Put some cool earth in a saucer and some water in another saucer and see how this works. Put both saucers in the sun. In about half an hour the surface of the soil will feel warm, but the water will still feel cool. Test the temperature with a thermometer.

Water doesn't heat as rapidly as the earth. When warm air over the land rises, the cooler air over the water comes in to take its place. This creates an onshore breeze, and as you know, it's much cooler nearer a lake or the ocean than the city.

Like the soil in the saucer, the land is heated by the sun and it becomes warmer than the water. The land heats the air above it and this warm air rises. Cooler air from nearby water moves in to take its place and creates a movement of air called an onshore breeze.

When the sun goes down, the land cools off. The water is now warmer than the land and warms the air above it. The warm air over the water begins to rise. Cooler air from over the land moves out to take its place. This movement of air is called an offshore breeze.

During the day, it is the land which *heats* faster than the water. But when the sun goes down, it is the land that also *cools* faster than the water. When the warmer air over the water rises, the cooler air from the land rushes in to take its place. This creates an offshore breeze.

Do winds change direction?

At night things change. Soil and rock, which heat faster than water, cool off faster than water. If you remove the top layer from the saucer of soil, you will find the soil that is left is still cool. The water is also cool, but not much cooler down deep than on the surface. The rays of the sun only hit the surface of soil and rock. The same rays go deep into water and heat it to a depth of several feet.

WATER YOU CAN'T SEE

What happens when water "dries up"?

WHEN we say that a pond has dried up we mean that the water in it has disappeared. What happened to it? The tiny bits or molecules which make up water have jumped into the air and are bouncing and bumping about with the molecules of air. We say the pond water has *evaporated* and we call water carried by the air "water vapor." The amount of water in the air varies at different times, but there is probably a quart or more of water in the air in your bedroom.

This picture illustrates evaporation taking place in a pond. The water is "drying up." Actually, the molecules of water bounce up toward the sky. The water carried along by the air is called water vapor.

Water will evaporate faster when it is exposed to the sun than when it is placed in the shade.

What causes evaporation?

It is heat which causes the water to evaporate or disappear into the air. All day long, water from ponds, rivers, lakes, oceans, puddles, plants and animals is heated by the sun and evaporates. The hotter it is, the quicker the water evaporates. You can test this by taking two saucers of the same size and putting a spoonful of water in each one. Place one saucer where it is warm and the other where it is cool. The water in the warmer place will dry up first. The water in this saucer has evaporated.

Wind helps to speed evaporation. If you blow on a wet piece of paper, or hold it out in the wind, it dries more quickly than a wet piece placed where the air is still. When you try this, it is best to wet one piece of paper and tear it in half so that one piece is just as wet as the other.

More water will evaporate from a large surface than a small one. A saucer with a spoonful of water spread over its bottom will dry up faster than the same amount of water left in the spoon.

Water evaporates more quickly when the air is dry. On a hot, dry day, perspiration evaporates quickly and your body is always dry. But if the air on a hot day is very moist, perspiration tends to stay on your body and you feel wet and uncomfortable.

Water evaporates faster when it is spread over a large surface than when it is contained in a small area.

Water molecules from the grass and soil will evaporate and form water vapor in a glass which has been placed upside down on the grass on a sunshiny day.

THE WATER CYCLE

What makes your window cloud up?

WHEN you take a water glass and place it upside down on the grass while the sun is shining brightly, something happens to that glass. A watery film begins to form on its sides. The outside of the glass is dry, but if you run your finger around the inside, you will find that it is wet. Molecules of water from the grass and soil have evaporated. They have become water vapor. Some of these vapor molecules have been cooled and slowed down as they hit against the side of the glass. Tens of thousands of them have joined together to form fine drops of water.

The same thing happens in a car on a cold day. Your warm breath strikes the cold windshield and the molecules stick to the windshield in the same kind of watery film. Have you ever seen this happen to the windows of your house on a cold day? And did any of the drops ever get so big that they ran down the windowpane? Perhaps you have seen this happen to a glass of ice water or a cold bottle of soda.

Does water go round in circles?

But if water keeps evaporating all the time, why doesn't everything dry up? Everything doesn't dry up because of a weather system called the water cycle.

Your experiment with the glass placed upside down on the grass helps tell you where the water goes.

The first step in the water cycle is called evaporation. Water from soil and grass *evaporated* inside your glass. The second step is *condensation*. Condensation happens when water vapor begins to form tiny drops which we can see as fog or clouds. A cloudy film *condensed* on the inside of your glass. The third step is called *precipitation*. Precipitation takes place when water returns to earth in the form of rain or snow. As larger drops form in your glass, they may become large enough to fall back to the ground. If this happens, it is "raining" inside your glass.

The three steps in the water cycle are *evaporation, condensation* and *precipitation*. The sun heats the water. Water vapor rises and forms clouds. The water returns to earth when it rains.

TINY SPECKS OF MANY THINGS

What floats in the air invisibly?

IF YOU look around the room you are in, the air might look very clear to you. But there are millions of tiny specks in the air you do not see. You would need a microscope to see most of them. Smoke from factory chimneys, pollen from flowers, salt spray and ordinary household dust all help fill the air with these tiny specks. Next time you see sunlight streaming through your window, look into the stream of light. This is the air you thought was clear. Just look at the number of small particles floating in that stream. What have all these specks to do with weather?

The air is full of specks, which you can see in a beam of sunlight streaming through a window.

WHAT IS A CLOUD?

Can you see water in the air when it isn't raining?

WHEN air becomes cooler, water vapor condenses around the little specks in the air you saw in the stream of sunlight. Millions and millions of tiny droplets, like the one which made the film of water on the inside of the glass, are formed. But now the watery film is high above you in the sky. Millions of these droplets, too small to fall, cluster together in groups. These are the clouds we see in the sky. Sometimes the clouds look fat and puffy because the sun is shining through them, making them white and bright. Perhaps you have tried to pick out different shapes or imagine cloud pictures as they float by.

Sometimes the sky looks like one big cloud. This is because there are so many layers of clouds that they block out part of the sun's rays. The day is gray and cloudy.

Sometimes when clouds form very, very high in the sky, where it is much colder, these droplets freeze. Then these tiny bits of ice float in the air and look like wispy ribbons from where you watch them.

Condensation takes place when water vapor rises and forms tiny drops which we can see as clouds.

Can you walk through a cloud?

But when water droplets form at ground level, these clouds are called fog. You are walking through a cloud when you walk through fog, and you can feel the dampness of these tiny droplets on your hands and face.

On a very cold day, you form a little cloud every time your moist breath hits the cold air.

Clouds are made of millions of tiny drops of water which float in the air.

DEW AND FROST

When does dew form?

AT NIGHT, when the soil, rocks and plants cool off, the layer of air which hugs the ground is cooled, too. Water vapor in the cooled air condenses as it touches the cooler soil and rocks and makes them wet. Tiny drops of water form on blades of grass and other plants. These tiny drops are dewdrops. If you get up early in the morning, you can see dewdrops sparkling in the sun. You must get up very early to see them, because when the air grows warmer, the dew evaporates and disappears into the air.

What is frost?

On very cold nights the water vapor condenses directly into ice crystals. The crystals form a white film on the ground and this film is frost.

You can make your own frost. Soak the label off a gallon paint can and pack the can with alternating layers of crushed ice and rock salt. Put in four cups of ice and then two cups of rock salt. Keep repeating this layer of ice and layer of rock salt until the can is full. Now let it stand and watch what happens. Some of the water vapor in the air will condense directly into ice crystals and form a thin layer of white frost all over the outside of the can. This is the way ice cream is chilled in home freezers.

Crushed ice and rock salt are the ingredients you need in order to make frost. Frost occurs when water vapor changes into little ice crystals.

WHAT COMES OUT OF THE SKY?

Why does it rain?

HOW hot or cold the air is makes a big difference in what kind of weather comes out of the sky.

It takes only a little increase in the temperature of the air to make a cloud disappear. The droplets of water evaporate and can no longer be seen. But if the air gets colder, larger drops are formed. When they become too heavy to float in the air, they fall to earth, just as the drops of water did when they ran down inside your glass. This is rain.

Is snow frozen rain?

When the air high in the sky cools very quickly, the water vapor condenses directly into crystals and you have a snowstorm. It is not true that snow is frozen rain. Snow is water vapor which condenses directly into ice crystals, the same way ice crystals formed on the can packed with ice and salt.

Do you know that every snowflake that falls is different from every other snowflake except for one thing? Every snowflake has six sides. No two are ever alike in design except for the six sides or points. Try to examine snowflakes. Look at them through a magnifying glass. They're even prettier seen this way than they are when you watch them falling silently on a winter day.

What should you call frozen rain?

When rain or partly melted snow freezes as it falls to earth, it is called sleet. Rain freezes into hard, clear little pellets of ice and the partly melted snow freezes into soft, milky pellets.

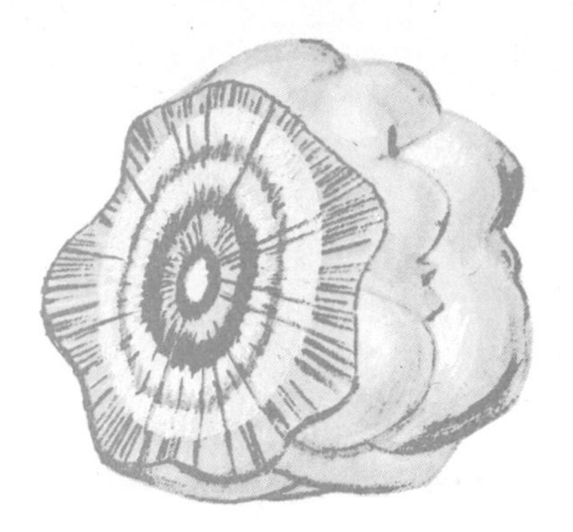

This cross-section of a hailstone shows its layers.

A snowflake is either a single ice crystal or made up of many crystals. In the center of each flake, there is a tiny particle, usually a speck of dust.

Of what are hailstones made?

There is something else which starts in the sky as one thing and lands on earth as something else. It is hail. Hail starts as rain, but before the drops of water can fall very far, the wind blows them high up in the air where it is colder. They freeze and start to fall again. Over and over they fall and are blown back again. Each time they fall, a new layer of water vapor condenses on them, and each time they are blown up into the freezing layer of air, this new layer of water turns to ice. Finally, the stone becomes too heavy to be lifted by the wind, and it falls to earth. Some hailstones have fallen which were as large as baseballs. but usually they are not much bigger than a small pea.

Next time you are in a hailstorm, pick up a few pieces of hail and cut them in half. Inside, you can see the layers that were formed as the hailstones fell, collected more moisture and were swept back up into the freezing air again. If you count the layers, you can tell how many trips each hailstone made before it finally fell and you picked it up.

FIREWORKS IN THE SKY

Can you identify a thundercloud?

WHEN the sun shines and there is a cool breeze blowing, this is one of weather's pleasant faces. But just as you sometimes frown, weather has its "frowning faces," too. One of these, which you see quite often in summertime, and occasionally in the winter, is the thunderstorm. It's noisy and loud and wet, but it can be just as exciting to watch from a safe place as Fourth of July fireworks.

A thundercloud is usually one which is flat on the bottom and towers in the sky with a top shaped something like an anvil. Strong currents of air range up and down as sudden winds warn us that the storm is about to break.

What causes lightning?

Lightning is electricity — the kind which sometimes causes a shock when you shuffle your feet on a carpet and then touch something made of metal, like a doorknob or a key.

As water droplets are rubbed and pulled about, they are charged with electricity. Suddenly the electric charge in one part of a cloud is attracted to a charge in another part of the same cloud or in another cloud. As it shoots through the air, it causes the air to glow

A thundercloud. Note the flat bottom and the top part which looks like a blacksmith's anvil.

for an instant and we see a lightning flash.

You can make your own lightning. All you need are two small balloons shaped like sausages. Blow them up and tie knots in the ends. Now you are ready to make lightning, but you must do this experiment in a room which is completely dark.

Rub the balloons back and forth against your trousers or dress, or the covering of a chair or sofa. Rub both balloons at the same time. Then bring them together so that they almost touch. You will see small flashes of light as the electricity jumps between the balloons and you will hear a faint crackle. You can do this over and over again.

Try making your own lightning with two balloons by following the directions on this page.

The powerful heat from lightning causes the great air or shock waves called thunder.

What causes thunder?

Outdoors, when electric currents flash through the air, the air is heated and expands rapidly. This sets a giant air wave in motion which we hear a few moments later as the roar of thunder. But light travels so fast that you see the flash at once, even before you hear the clap of thunder.

Since it takes sound about five seconds to travel one mile, you can tell how many miles you are from the lightning by dividing by five the number of seconds it takes from the time you see the lightning until you hear the thunder. For example, if you hear the thunder four seconds after you see the lightning, the flash occurred just 4/5 of a mile away.

THE STORM WITH AN EYE

THERE is another storm which is much more dangerous than a thunderstorm. You wouldn't like to be caught in this storm because it does a great deal of damage before it fades away. It is called a hurricane.

Where do hurricanes come from?

Hurricanes are storms born over tropical waters. The blazing sun beats down on the ocean waters day after day and the air above this water grows very hot. Suddenly cold air moves in from many directions. It pushes this hot air straight up until the hot air reaches a cool layer of air. The water vapor condenses very suddenly and becomes a driving rain. Cooler air from the outside moves in, in a whirling motion, like water going down a drain. The center or "eye" of the hurricane is calm, but all around it the winds and rain are swirling.

How strong is a hurricane?

Hurricanes last for several days as the storm whirls onward in its fury. It creates enormous waves which flood the land and the winds are strong enough to knock houses into a pile of wood and tear big trees up by the roots.

Cold air moving in from many directions, as the arrows indicate, is a step in the formation of a hurricane.

SKY PICTURES

What changes the way the sky looks?

THE SKY around you is like a giant picture which keeps changing as the weather changes.

Sometimes the picture has a blue sky with large white clouds floating peacefully through space.

Sometimes the picture is a dark one with deep gray clouds and rain.

Sometimes the sky picture is a sunrise like a red glow in the early morning.

You watch a different picture when you watch the sun set in the west among purple clouds. Each sunset is different. Your picture changes every day.

Where must the sun be when you look at a rainbow?

Once in a while, almost like a special occasion, you'll see a rainbow in your sky picture. If the sun shines through the clouds while it is still raining, as it sometimes does in summer showers, a band of many colors seems to bend across the sky. You'll miss seeing it if you face the sun. A rainbow can only be seen if the sun is at your back.

If you'd like to make tiny rainbows of your own, you might dip the top of a soda bottle into soapy water so that a film forms across the opening. Take the bottle into the sunlight so that light passes through the curved glass and strikes the soapy film. Can you see lots of colors? These are rainbow colors.

WEATHER INSTRUMENTS

THERMOMETER: When mercury in the bulb at the bottom of the thermometer tube becomes hotter, it expands and rises up the glass tube. As it cools, it contracts and drops down. The numbers on the scale show the temperature in degrees.

WIND VANE: It is used to find the direction of the wind. The arrow points to the direction from which the wind is coming. This direction gives the wind its name.

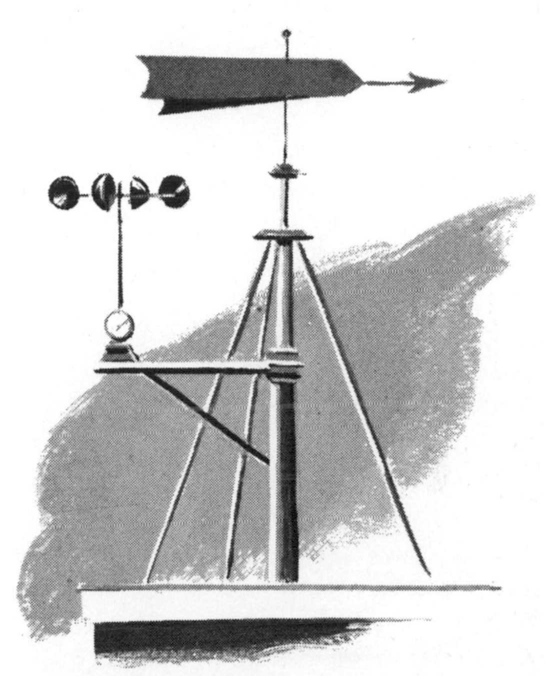

ANEMOMETER: The cups "catch" the wind and spin at varying speeds, faster or slower, depending upon the wind's speed.

ANEROID BAROMETER: It is used to measure atmospheric pressure. A needle is connected to an airless metal box. Air pressure on the top of the box moves the needle.

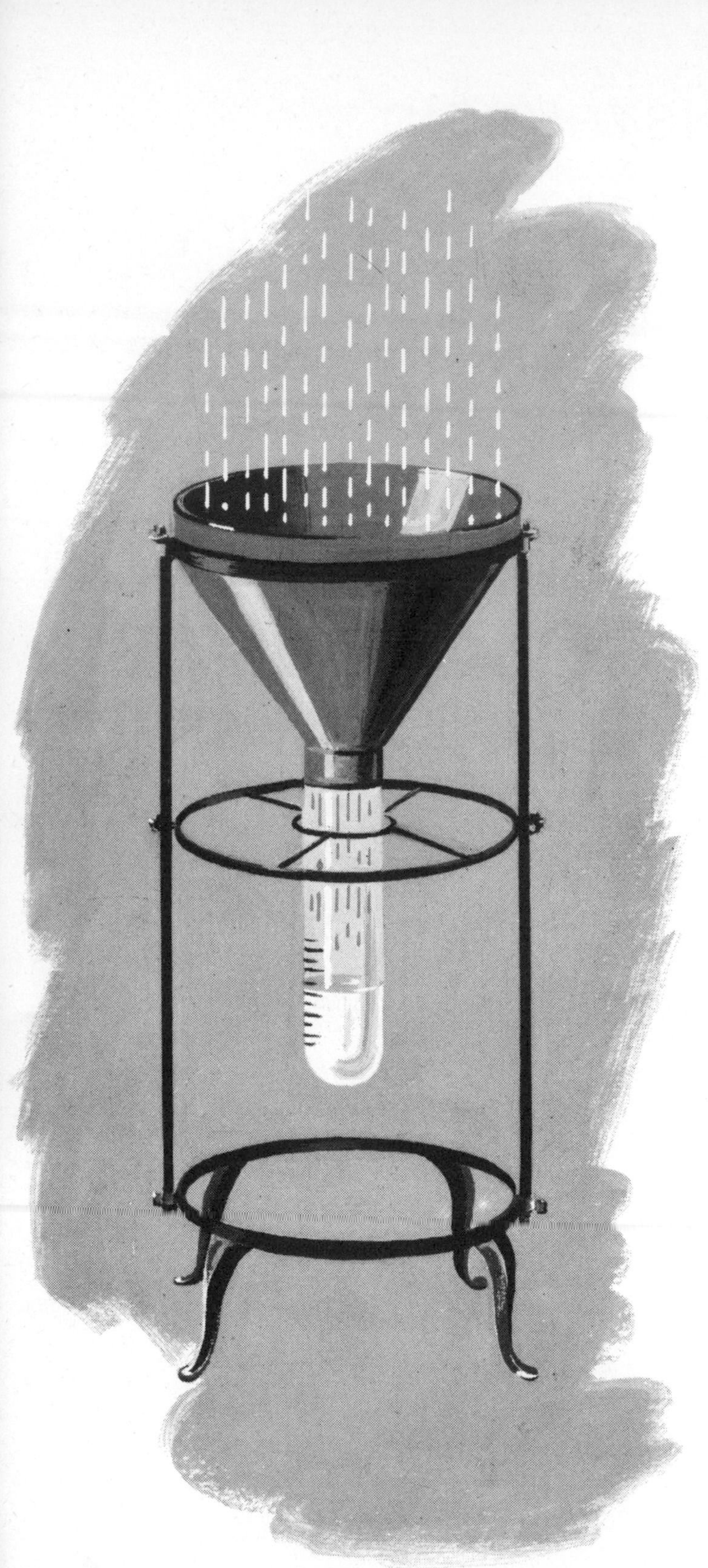

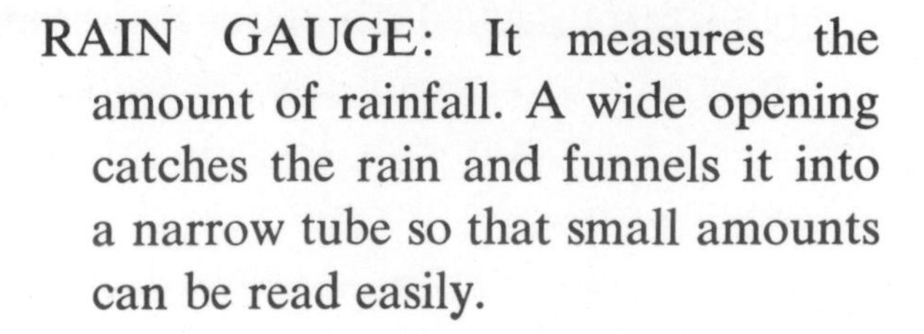

RAIN GAUGE: It measures the amount of rainfall. A wide opening catches the rain and funnels it into a narrow tube so that small amounts can be read easily.

CLOUD DIRECTION INDICATOR (NEPHOSCOPE): This shows the direction of clouds by reflection. The direction of the wind high in the sky is often different from the direction of the wind near the ground.

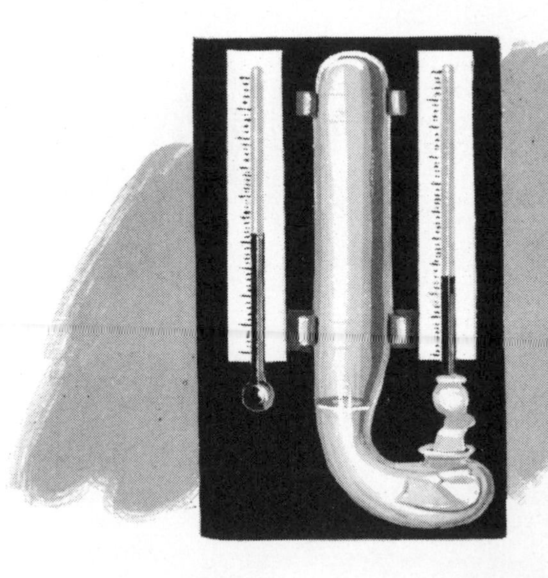

HYGROMETER: A moist cloth is wrapped around the bulb of a thermometer. The moisture content of the air is measured by the rate of evaporation, which cools the thermometer. An ordinary dry bulb thermometer and a chart are used to determine relative humidity.

CLIMATE

IN THIS book you have been reading about the types of weather in the northern hemisphere, where you live, because this weather makes our climate. But different parts of the world have different weather. They are in different climates. You know how important weather is to you and the way you live. It's important to other people, too, who live in other places. And it is important to the plants and animals that grow and live in these places.

Here is the earth sliced in two, with bands drawn to show the different climates. One side shows the plants that grow and the other side shows the animals living in these different climates.

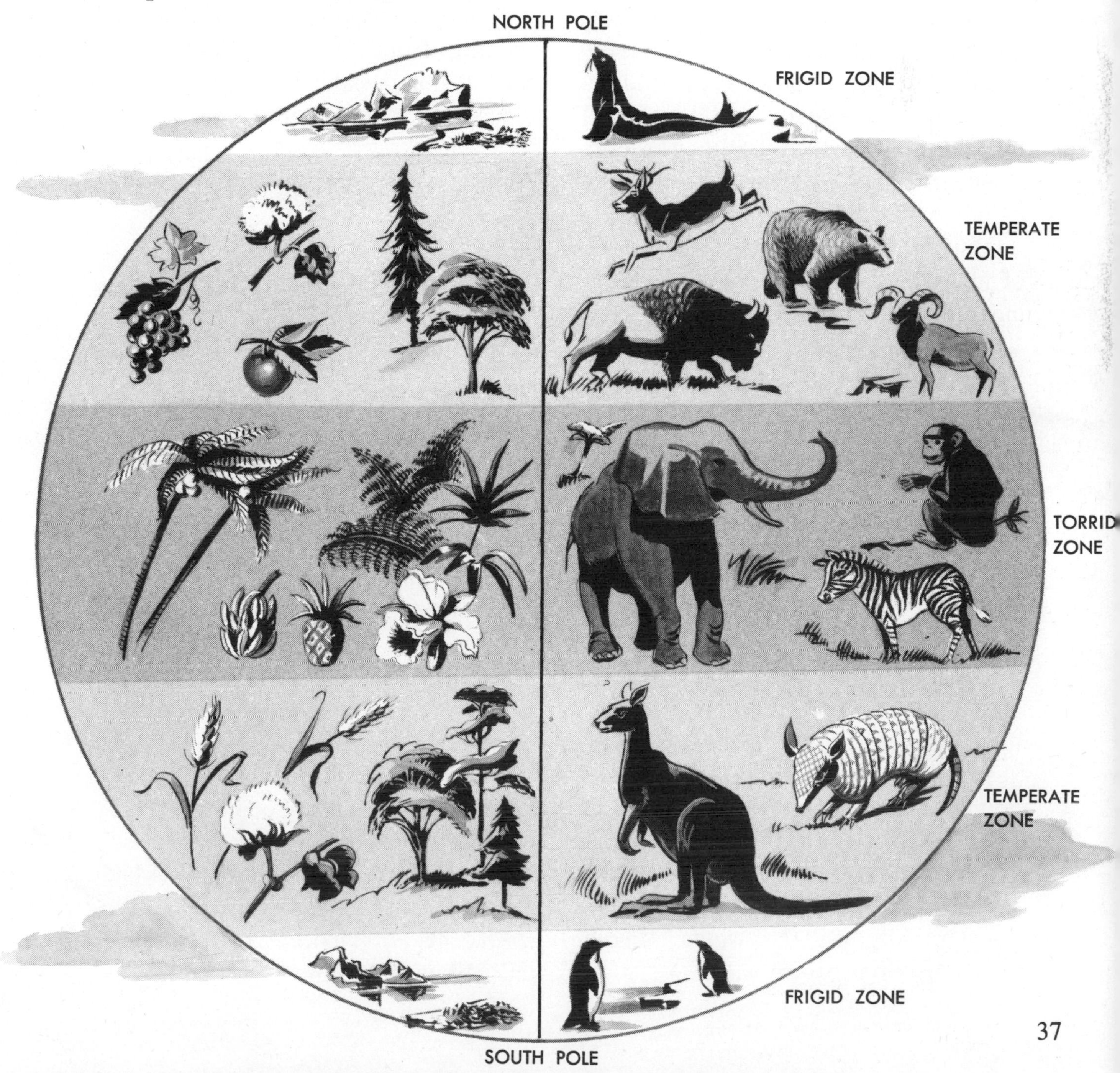

TYPES OF CLOUDS

CUMULUS

Cumulus is a Latin word which means "heap." These puffy white clouds heap up in thick masses. Shaped like a dome on the top and flat on the bottom, they look like mountains in the sky. Cumulus clouds often form on hot summer afternoons and are usually 4,000 to 5,000 feet above the earth. When they become thick and heavy with water, cumulus clouds may develop into thunderheads or thunderclouds, so that the presence of many of them in the sky may often mean that it is going to rain.

CIRRUS

Cirrus is a Latin word which means "curl" or "ringlet." Cirrus clouds, forming high in the sky, are feathery wisps of curly white ice crystals. These delicate clouds, which appear in dry weather, form at an altitude of from five to ten miles above the ground. They are the highest clouds in the sky and move along rapidly on the winds. Cirrus clouds are often storm warnings.

STRATUS

Stratus is also a Latin word and means "spreading out." This describes the great width of these foglike clouds. They appear at low altitudes, generally ranging from 2,000 to 7,000 feet. Spread out in calm flat layers, stratus clouds often mean bad weather ahead.

NIMBUS

Nimbus is a Latin word meaning "rainstorm," and so, nimbus clouds are rain clouds. These dark gray clouds do not have any definite shape and appear at low altitudes over a wide area of the sky.

Weather scientists use these names to describe the main cloud formations. They also use combinations of these words, such as *cirro-stratus, strato-cumulus* and *cumulo-nimbus. Cirro-stratus,* for example, means a spread-out layer of cirrus clouds. People who study weather use other words to classify clouds, such as the word *alto,* which means "high." The combinations *alto-stratus* or *alto-cumulus,* for example, tell us how high these clouds are.

THE BEAUFORT SCALE

MANY years ago, before modern weather instruments were used, a man named Sir Francis Beaufort made up a scale to describe the force of winds by the way they acted over land and sea. Here is a form of this scale. How many of these wind effects have you felt? Scale numbers indicate wind strength.

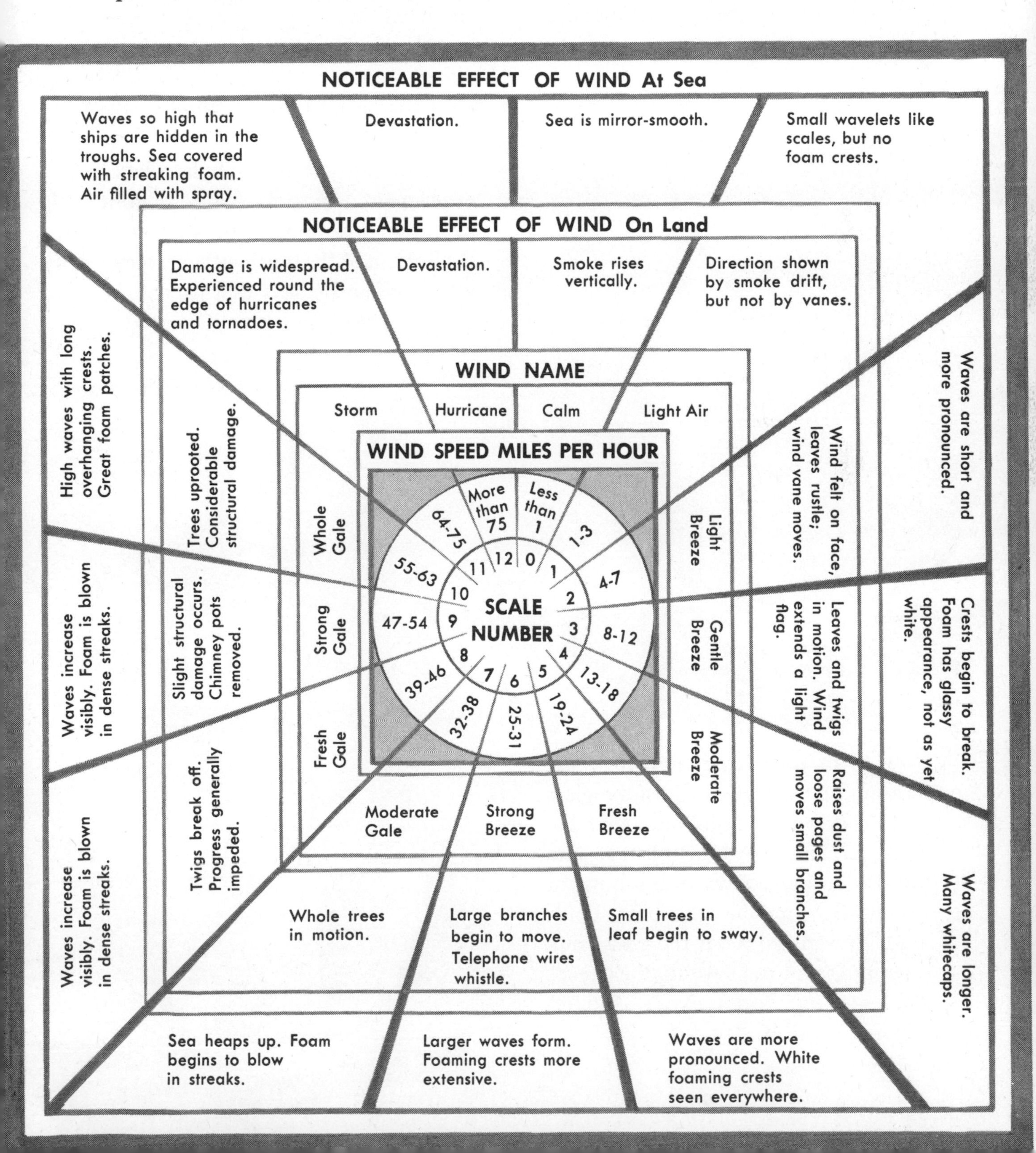

MORE WEATHER EXPERIMENTS

1. If you tried turning a glass upside down and pushing it straight down into a bowl of water as suggested on page 6, you might now try these experiments.

(a) Push your handkerchief to the bottom of a dry glass. Turn the glass upside down (making sure that the handkerchief stays in place), and push it straight down into a bowl of water. Be sure that the bowl holds enough water to cover the glass completely. You can prove that air keeps the water out, because your handkerchief will still be dry.

(b) Do the same experiment except that, instead of a handkerchief, a cork can be floated on the water in the bowl. When you press the open mouth of the glass down into the water, the pocket of air will force the cork to the bottom. As long as the glass is full of air, the water can't get in. You can use this simple science experiment as a trick. Ask a friend if he knows how to make the cork go to the bottom of the bowl without touching it. When he says that it can't be done — show him that it can!

(c) If you push an upside-down glass straight down into your bowl of water and then tilt it slightly, some of the air will get out and bubble up to the surface. Now try another stunt. Use a large pan of water, such as a dishpan, and push into it two upside-down glasses, until both are completely under water. Tilt one glass so that all of the air bubbles to the surface. One glass will now be full of water, and the other full of air. Raise them so that the open ends of the glasses remain beneath the water, but most of the glasses are out of it, as shown in the picture. Then move the glass full of air so that an edge is under the glass full of water, tipping it so that the air bubbles up into the glass full of water. As the air from one glass bubbles into the other, the glass full of water will become filled with air and the glass which was filled with air will now be filled with water. If you are careful, you can keep pouring the air back and forth from one glass to the other. The glass may be filled with either air or water, but not both. Air, like water, is real, and two real things cannot fill the same space at the same time.

2. On page 7 you discovered that air has weight — the weight of a column of air several miles high. We call this weight "pressure" and it pushes in all directions. Here are a few more experiments to show how this works.

(a) Cut from a cereal box (or any lightweight cardboard) a piece large enough to cover the top of a drinking glass. Fill the glass with water. Holding the card tightly on top of the glass, turn the glass upside down. Then hold on to the glass with one hand and take the other hand away from the card. What makes the card stay in place and hold the water in the glass? It is the pressure of the air which pushes out in every direction. If you hold the glass sideways, the card still stays on. (It is best to do this experiment over a sink or tub, just in case of accident.)

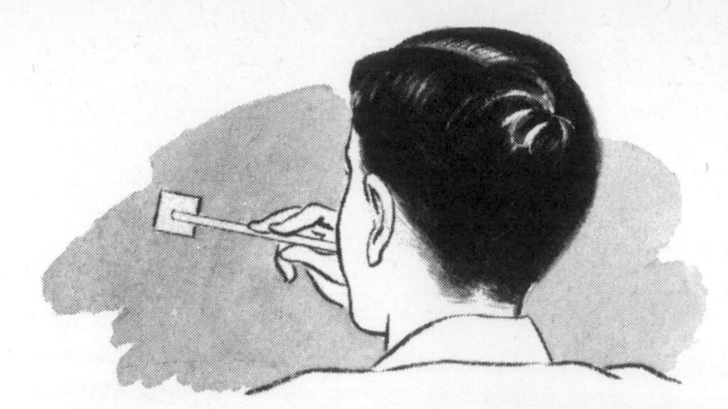

(b) Hold a straw in your hand. Like the pressure within your body, the air pressure inside the straw is the same as the pressure on the outside. Now cut out a piece of paper about one inch square. Hold it against one end of the straw and suck through the other end. As long as you keep sucking, the paper will remain in place at the end of the straw, even after you remove your hand. The reason this happens is that as you suck air from the straw, the inside air pressure becomes less than that outside the straw. The outside pressure pushing the paper at the end of the straw holds it in place.

(c) Next use the straw to drink from a glass of water. What happens? As you suck on the straw, the pressure inside the straw becomes less than the pressure pushing down against the water, and so it pushes the water up through the straw and into your mouth.

(d) Take the same straw and hold a finger over one end. Push the other end straight down into a glass of water. You will see a little water go up into the straw from the bottom as the air in the straw compresses a little. But it will not keep going up into the straw. As with the upside-down glass which was pushed straight down into the water in experiment 1(a), the water cannot enter the straw while the air is kept in. Now take your finger away from the end of the straw and you will see the water rise into the straw until it reaches the level of the rest of the water in the glass. When this happens, some of the air inside the straw is pushed out through the top. Place your finger on the end of the straw again and lift the straw out of the glass. The water will stay in the straw. No air can come in the top and the air pressing up at the bottom is strong enough to hold the water in. When you take away your finger again, the air presses down from the top with as much force as it presses up from the bottom and the weight of the water causes it to drop from the straw. The same method is used with larger glass tubes for removing tiny fish and other objects from tanks of water. Such tubes are called "dip tubes."

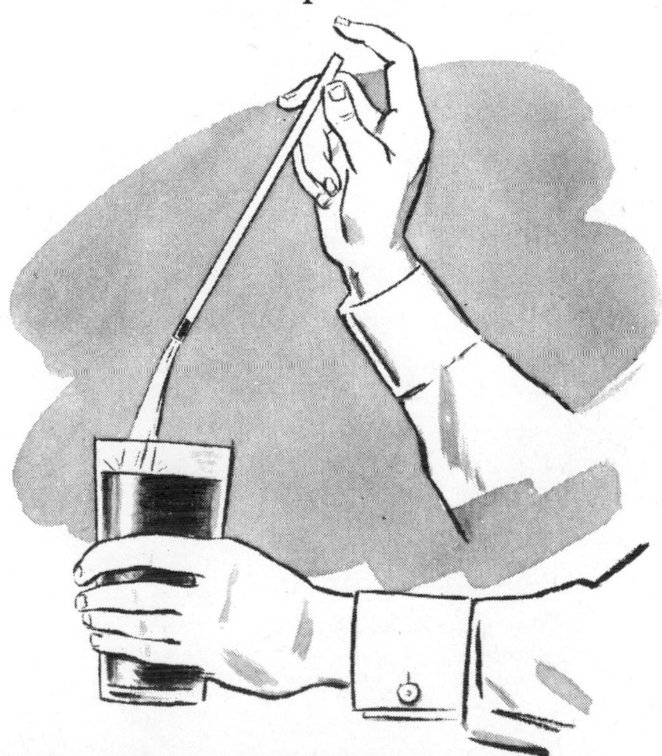

3. On page 9 you learned how molecules move about. High up, where the air is thinner, there are fewer molecules to bump against each other and heat up. Nearer to the earth, where the molecules are squeezed close together, they collide more often and become hotter. Try this experiment to show what happens.

(a) Fill a balloon with dried navy beans. Then blow it up and hold it at the neck so that the air cannot escape. Shake the balloon lightly. The beans will bounce about like air molecules which are always on the move. As they bounce back and forth, they will bump into one another and you will hear a little click. The more beans you are able to squeeze into the balloon before it is blown up, the more clicks there will be. And so you can see how molecules of air, squeezed together close to the earth, rub against each other more often — and how they become hotter, as the molecules of your skin do when you rub your hands back and forth quickly.

4. The fact that dark colors absorb more heat than light colors was explained on page 10. Try another experiment to prove this scientific principle.

(a) Use two white paper drinking cups. Paint one of them black. Fill both with water of the same temperature and place them in the sun. After thirty to forty minutes, test the temperature of the water in each one. (An ordinary weather or cooking thermometer will do for this purpose.) Which is warmer?

5. Air expands when it is heated. This is shown by the experiment described on page 16. Here is another interesting experiment to show that this is so.

(a) Snap the neck of a balloon around an empty quart-sized soda bottle. Since there will be very little air in the balloon, it will droop to one side. Run water from the cold water tap against the side of the bottle. Even the little bit of air which was in the balloon will seem to leave it and it will be even limper than it was in the beginning. Next, run hot water against the side of the bottle and the balloon will begin to expand with air. No air could either enter or leave the balloon. What happened? The answer is that air takes up less space when it is cold and more space when it is hot. The cold water cooled the air inside the bottle so that it took up less space than when the balloon was first put over the neck of the bottle. The hot water then heated the air in the bottle so that it took up more room and caused the air to force its way into the balloon which was able to stretch.

Hot air is lighter than cold air and therefore rises. But then, does cold air fall? Try this experiment.

(b) Get a small piece of dry ice and place it carefully in a shallow saucer of water near the edge of a table. Cold air will bubble from the saucer and you can watch it drop down to the floor. It is because cold air falls that it is possible to leave freezers uncovered in supermarkets.

6. Whether it is inside a house, as you read about on page 17, or the tornadoes and winds you read about on pages 18-20, hot air always rises and cold air comes in to take its place. You can show how this happens in a simple kitchen experiment.

(a) Sometime when your mother is using the burners on the stove, make sure that the windows and doors to the kitchen are closed. Open the door of the refrigerator and ask your mother to hold a burning match or candle at the bottom of the refrigerator opening. Notice that the cold air is falling from the refrigerator and carries the smoke down. Next, ask her to hold the match or candle halfway between the refrigerator and the stove, about a foot from the floor. Can you see the smoke moving in the direction of the stove? Now ask your mother to hold the match or candle over the stove. Watch the smoke go straight up. You have followed the course of a little breeze which you made in your own kitchen.

7. You read on pages 21 and 22 about evaporation. Your mother is especially interested in evaporation when she has clothes to dry. You can do some more experiments to find out when evaporation works best.

(a) Soak two handkerchiefs in water and hang them up to dry — one where it is sunny and the other in the shade. Which dries first?

(b) Soak two handkerchiefs in water and hang them up to dry — one open and one folded twice. Which dries first?

THE WEATHER — SEEN FROM SPACE

MANY man-made satellites have been put into orbit around the earth since the Space Age began. Of these, a good number have been weather satellites, designed to provide meteorologists — the scientists who study weather and climate — with an overall picture of atmospheric conditions. The information received, in turn, enables them to forecast the weather in specific areas with greater accuracy and to warn people of impending storms.

The first of the orbiting satellites to send weather information back to earth was the *Vanguard II,* launched on February 17, 1959. On April 1, 1960, *Tiros I* was launched — it was the first satellite to actually take pictures of the earth's weather in detail. *Tiros II,* launched on November 23 of the same year, measured infrared rays given off by the earth and also took weather pictures. And *Tiros III,* launched on July 12, 1961, was the first one to discover a hurricane — Hurricane Esther — over the Atlantic Ocean. Early warnings went out to those in the storm's probable path.

Further developments came about with the launchings of subsequent *Tiros* satellites, including the measurement of temperature and electron density in space. (The launching of *Tiros X,* in the summer of 1965, concluded this particular series.)

Another hurricane—Hurricane Dora — was progressively tracked off the coast of Florida by *Nimbus I,* a weather satellite launched on August 28, 1964. *Nimbus II* (launched May 15, 1966) measured the earth's heat balance.

The need for a world-wide network of trained weather observers who would join together in a program leading to improved weather forecasts and, eventually, weather control, was recognized by President John F. Kennedy in a speech before the United Nations on September 25, 1961.

An appropriate plan was drawn up, and by the following summer, the World Weather Watch, directed by the World Meteorological Organization (WMO), an agency of the United Nations, came into being.

The purposes of the World Weather Watch include keeping the earth's atmosphere under observation, transmitting weather information to all nations, and improving forecasting services. In the United States, the facilities of the Environmental Science Services Administration (ESSA), of which the Weather Bureau is an important part, are charged with this responsibility. The Tiros Operational Satellite (TOS) system began in February, 1966, with the launching of *ESSA I,* a weather satellite that photographs clouds, stores the information on magnetic tape, and then telemeters it to ground stations, where it is "fed" directly to a computer. The computer is capable of reproducing a picture of the cloud pattern as it then exists over all the world. The following TOS satellite, *ESSA II,* was equipped with an automatic picture-transmission system that sent pictures to receiver-recorders on the ground every 208 seconds.

Other specialized weather satellites are the Applications Technology Satellites (shortened to ATS). *ATS-I* was launched on December 6, 1966, its speed adjusted to the speed of the earth at the equator so that it remains over the same position on earth, in this case, over the Line Islands in the Pacific Ocean. It is equipped with a device which works like a camera, but which is more accurately a "pinhole-type" scanning telescope that transmits electronic pulses (translated from observed cloud formations) to a computer on the ground. A more sophisticated ATS, *ATS-III,* was launched and positioned over the Amazon River in Brazil on November 5, 1967. It transmits color pictures of half the earth every thirty minutes.

The Global Atmospheric Research Program (GARP) is another international project that will pursue greater meteorological knowledge throughout the 1970's. Balloons, buoys, satellites and airplanes will all gather information which will be computer processed at such a fast rate that long-range predictions of the weather will be both accurate and reliable. This will come about as scientists learn more about the interaction of air with the land and the oceans, and about the physics of our atmosphere that gains and loses heat by radiation.